39 Things About Life I Learned In Prison:

Turn My Mistake Into Your Success

Edward Ball

Ball Team Enterprise LLC

Published by:
Ball Team Enterprise LLC
© 2013 by Edward Ball

eBook ISBN: 978-0-9899864-0-3

Paper back ISBN: 978-0-9899864-2-7

Table of Contents

You Must Have Something Greater Than

***

This is dedicated to my momma for giving me my...

Introduction

In life we will all be blessed with opportunities to learn lessons. These opportunities to learn arise in every aspect of our lives; both the complex and the simple aspects offer chances to learn lessons about our existence. However, not many of us take time or have the ability to extract life lessons from these opportunities. For example, does anyone wrest a lesson from a simple situation like riding a bike? Probably not. However, in order to ride a bike you must reach out and grab the handle bars. For your relationships to be successful, you must reach out.

I learned many things about life while in prison. I had the time and motivation to make sense out of everything that took place around me. Some things I outline were actually learned prior to going to prison, however, I didn't understand them at the time. Prison experiences helped me to actually learn lessons previously taught. This book is a small compilation of some things I learned about life while in prison.

Some may ask why 39 lessons? This number is significant because it ran through my head for many years. When I was sent off to prison on four separate cases and around 10 violent felonies, I had a 39-year prison sentence to do. For each year the state of Indiana gave me, I am going to give my readers one lesson that I learned in prison.

I begin each chapter with a title that represents a lesson I learned. Then I go on to explain the title/lesson. Then I tell you how I came to learn the lesson under the subtitle called life lessons. I like to keep things short, sweet and easy for consumption, so I wrap up the chapters using a quotable one or two-liner that sums up at least one point I attempted to make in the chapter. As some supplemental information I have a couple of action steps that someone can take to either avoid the situation or mistake I made or to improve themselves personally or professionally.

Caveat: I went to prison at a young age. I have seen and learned many things that are abnormal to mainstream society. As a result my take on life and my interpretation of complex and simple situations may be warped. If nothing else they may be interesting, hopefully they will be helpful.

***

Tom Cat Taught Me That...

Nonsense Thoughts Lead to Nonsense Situations

What we do is an expression of what we are thinking. Those actions stemming from our thoughts create situations. If we constantly think about Nonsense we will constantly and consistently find ourselves in Nonsense situations.

I believe what we think about will eventually manifest from something intangible to something tangible. In other words, our thoughts will go from being just thoughts that can't be seen or felt to something viewable, touchable and corporeal.

Thoughts swirling around in our mind are something private, intimate and powerful. The intimacy and privacy of our thoughts is evident in that they are part of us like a child inside a mother's womb growing without a protruding stomach as an indicator of its existence. The power of our thoughts is seen once they become an action and a result. The action is a result of a single powerful thought and the situation you find yourself in, after the act is carried out, is a result of the thought and the consequent action.

The things you think about play a significant role in the situations you find yourself in. If you constantly think about drugs, you will eventually find yourself in drug related situations whether it is a drug deal or a drug bust. If you constantly think about women you will find yourself in the midst of women sooner or later. Your thoughts compel you to act. I can't sit on a thought for too long without getting up and acting on that thought. For me, acting on the things running through my mind is like removing a bullet from the chamber of a gun…once that bullet is gone, I can put new thoughts in the chamber. If that thought goes without being acted upon, I can't load my mind's chamber with fresh thoughts and I become stuck. The danger lies in the type of thoughts I generate; if I generate Nonsense ones, I will find myself in Nonsense situations.

Life Lesson

When first incarcerated, I was in the county jail and still had the streets heavy on my mind. I was thinking about money, women, weed and putting in work. I eventually found myself in deadlock, a segregation unit in the Marion County Jail. From deadlock, I went to trial. In deadlock, you aren't allowed privileges like phone calls and the law library so I wasn't able to prepare for my trial and I was facing around 90-plus years. All this was a result of what I had on my mind.

After spending many years in prison I had the

opportunity to see and talk to many people. After a while you begin to be able to tell who will find themselves in messed up situations by simply talking to them. The ones who always had that nonsense on their minds always were in the secure housing unit (SHU), in lock fights, knife fights, race wars, drug rip-offs, drug busts, and any other kind of crazy circumstances that might occur in prison.

In the early 2000s, I went back to the county jail from maximum security prison. Another guy, named Tomcat, went back with me. You could tell by Tomcat's walk that he was on nonsense. He walked like those bullies in Tom and Jerry who lead the little gang wearing their little derbies. He walked with his fist balled up and arms bowed out at his side, as if his back was too wide to rest his arms at his side. He stuck his chests out like he was letting a visually impaired person read a very small tattoo on his pecks. From the time we left the cell house to the time we came back to the prison, about a week later, he had been in all kinds of messes. He was segregated from us as we dressed out to be transported to the jail because he wouldn't shut up, he wouldn't listen, and he tried to defy every rule in place. Once in the county he was taken out of the cell block he was housed in because of some gang related mess. This continued on for a week. He could not stay out of trouble. When I spoke with him all he had on his mind was nonsense; nothing positive or constructive ever fell out of his mouth. This is a guy who won an appeal on a 55-year sentence, was released, and came back to prison with a brand new 50-year sentence.

I learned from him and countless others in prison, including myself that the first step in staying out of trouble begins with what's in your mind. Every single person who constantly thought of only Nonsense found themselves in it. A few years after my deadlock experience I realized I needed to change what I was thinking about. As soon as I moved from thinking about money, trafficking, the streets, violence, revenge, and the sort but instead began thinking about education, success, freedom, sustainability, family, and my worth, I basically stayed out of trouble. All the things related to trouble no longer mattered. My thoughts turned into action, and I ended up with a couple of degrees, eight years knocked off my sentence, marketable skills, a better relationship with my family and a redefined sense of self-worth and my peers who were on that Nonsense are still at maximum security prisons. Both of our thoughts went from something intangible to something tangible. The difference is that my thoughts gave birth to something positive and theirs' resulted in some Nonsense!

Summary

If you want to change your situation for the better change your mind in the direction of better.

Action

1. Give your thoughts more consideration before you turn them to action

When that thought pops in your head think about what the possible results of acting on that thought will be. This is harder than it sounds so…

2. If you find yourself in a bad situation learn from it.

We often act without thinking. As a result, we find ourselves in predicaments. Once we are in a bad way we have to do more than try and find a way out. Take that opportunity to learn. Learn how you got there so you won't be back and learn how you moved on so you can not only duplicate it if you ever need to but so you can help others find their way also.

***

My 39-Year Prison Sentence Taught Me...

Don't Ask 'Why me?'

Things happen to everybody in some shape, form, fashion, time and space. Sometimes you are a winner, and other times you are a loser. I don't ask "Why me?" when I win, so I have learned not to ask "Why me?" when I am on the losing end. Instead of asking "Why me?" I try to find out "Why not me?"

Some people live great lives where everything goes right. One day something goes terribly wrong with that great life, and they are unable to understand why the terrible is happening to them and not someone else. Are they better than everyone else being subjected to tragedy? No! We are all mortal beings subject to the whims of fortune as well as calamity.

As we go through life, we make the mistake of thinking we deserve nothing but fortune and we never ask why we are receiving it. However, we have the impudence to ask "Why me?" when we experience the other side of the coin. I don't ask "Why me?" when I am doing well nor do I ask "Why me?" when things are all bad because I know why. I know why, because I have taken the time out to find out "Why me?" which allows me to instead ask "Why not me?"

The question "Why me?" is indicative of a lack of humility and understanding. Asking the question "Why me?" shows that you are arrogant. Arrogance causes one to believe that he or she shouldn't be subject to experiencing misfortune. It is also a sign that one lacks understanding. At the very least, an understanding of balance is missing or under developed. For example, if there is light there is darkness somewhere, if there is hunger somewhere there is gluttony and if someone is experiencing good there is someone somewhere experiencing the opposite. When you are winning somewhere out there is a loser, that's balance. If every day was a sunny day, life wouldn't be anything but a dessert. Balance ensures life is a mixture of sunny days and rainy ones.

Life Lesson

When I was sentenced and ended up in prison with nearly 40 years, I couldn't stop asking "Why me?" It seemed to be a question many of us inside prison were asking. After a few years of living with the violence, backstabbing, the conniving, the selfishness and all the aspects of the dark side of human nature, I began to ask "Why not me?" We almost deserved misfortune.

Humility is required to see that you are not above experiencing tragedy and misfortune. It takes humility to be honest about your deserving of some of the tragedy and misfortune you experience. Once I asked the question "Why not me?" I began eliminating many of the things in my life that contribute to me deserving bad while understanding that I am still at misfortune's mercy. Bad things happen to bad and good people alike.

I don't ask "Why me?" because doing so shows my lack of understanding and humility. I ask "Why not me?" instead because I am humble and honest enough to understand the role of my actions, the results of my actions, the capriciousness of calamity and balance in this life. I certainly didn't end up in a maximum security prison for nothing. That 39 years I received was disaster's whimsicality, and I am positive that when I lost my trial someone won theirs.

Asking 'Why not me' forces me to look at my actions whether they result in good or bad. After that analysis I can do more of the things that result in positive outcomes and do less of the things that result in negative ones. The "Why me?" question doesn't force similar analysis instead it allows for blame and entitlement; in other words, when you hear someone ask "Why me?" they are looking for someone to blame for their misfortune and feel as if they are entitled to luck.

Summary

If you ask "Why me?" you'll likely never find out, instead ask "Why not me?" and you'll begin to search for the answer, the former question is usually emblematic of self-importance and a lack of comprehension.

Action

1. Look at the things you have done in your life. Taking a look at what you have done during your life you should be able to determine what actions resulted in good and what actions had a negative outcome. Once that determination is made…

2. Begin doing more things that have positive outcomes and fewer things that have negative ones.

Positive outcomes aren't ephemeral. We mistake short-term positive outcomes as good things. We have long lives to live and need to have long-lasting and continuous positive results – not a short-lived positive result ending in years of negativity.

***

Lock-Down Facilities Taught Me That...

If You Look Long Enough You Will See Something Different.

Have you ever seen those pictures with dual images? Like the one with the old lady and the young lady? What or who you see depends on your initial perception. However, if you look at that image long enough you will see something different. This is true for the things in our life.

Some of us will live long enough to be able to take long looks at the things in our lives and our lives as a whole. In addition, we will be fortunate enough to have tools and references that will allow us to see those different things. Those tools include: hindsight, experience, understanding and discernment. When you have the opportunity to look back on things after they have occurred, you will usually see things differently. Experience allows us to see familiar situations differently the second time around. Understanding works in similar fashion. Once we understand a thing we look at it differently. References or things that can be used to make comparisons can help you see new things by propagating possibilities. For example, we have records set by one person and set out to be broken by another person. The record opens people's eyes to the possibility that more is possible. When we know that more is possible we begin to see things differently, which allow us to create records, break records, and come up with ways to make possibilities realities.

As we use the various tools we have at our disposal we are basically taking a long look at things. Instead of jumping in head first we take time to delve into our experience bank, our fountain of understanding and our register of discernment to see deeper into a thing and see it from various perspectives. This depth and variety of views gives us the opportunity to see this thing differently and gives us the opportunity to make a more optimal decision in relation to that thing. I liken what I am saying to being in the dessert and seeing a mirage. At first the mirage looks like fresh drinking water and is compelling you to expend energy to move closer to it. However, if we use our tools, stop and take a look at the mirage we will begin to see that it is an optical illusion. Once we begin to see the mirage differently we can make a decision to not waste time, energy and other resources moving in the direction of the illusion.

Life Lesson

The first two prisons I found myself in were basically lockdown facilities. We were locked in two-man cells from 18 to 24 hours a day. Under these circumstances, you have the chance to make sense of all sorts of things, the most important of which is your life and lifestyle.

Needless to say, I took a look at many aspects of my life, and I began to rethink many of my previous beliefs. I started looking at and seeing things differently. All the things I was involved in took on a new look, one that was less attractive.

Sitting in prison, I saw all types of individuals. The ones who struck chords with me were the youngsters that I saw myself in. Watching these youngsters made me ashamed and embarrassed because I realized how stupid I must have been and looked when I was them. I dressed the same, spoke the same, and adhered to the same nonsensical ideologies. I guess you could say that they opened my eyes and permitted me to see things in a totally new light.

With this seemingly new found ability to see things

differently, I applied it to other areas of my life and began making better, not yet optimal, decisions related to those areas. Despite what people think about prison, you can do many of the things you were doing on the streets. That is, you can thug just as hard, sell or use just as much dope, rob, steal and do nearly everything you once did that landed you in prison to begin with. Due to the way I was seeing things, I repudiated all those things and safely navigated through prison.

All the things I once did no longer made sense. It is crazy because even after being sentenced to nearly 40 years in the IDOC I still saw my street lifestyle in a positive light. It wasn't until I stared at it that I was able to see something different in my life and that life style. I truly believe that if I didn't use the resources I had to see something different I would still be in prison, a mental and physical one.

Summary

To do better, start by taking a better look and seeing

things as they truly are.

Action

1. Use your resources to see things from various angles.

You have the ability to put yourself in different positions, whether it is physically or mentally. That ability is one of your resources. People in your network can give you another angle or perspective on things. A different set of eyes may see entirely different due to the lenses they wear. Our experiences, beliefs, knowledge base and a host of other things creates our lenses.

2. Use the information gathered from these resources to make a better decision.

To make an optimal decision you must have information, preferably information from various angles. For example, when you are purchasing a car you walk around it, get inside, lift the hood, drive it, and do all that you can to see it from various points of view so you can be sure if you are making the right decision regarding purchasing the vehicle. Making other decisions should require a similar information gathering process and use of that information.

***

From the Ingenious Ideas of Convicts I Learned To...

Worry About What You Have Not About What You Don't

In the fall of 1999, I was sent to southern Indiana to begin what was, to me, a life sentence. The correctional facility I was sent to was like an asylum for dead men walking. In the winter it looked like barren tundra where men were sent to keep them from harming society and to eventually die.

In a place like the one I described, men begin to worry about all the things they don't have. I was focused on the things that made up my previous life. I couldn't stop thinking about clothes, women, friends and freedom.

Apparently I wasn't the only one. Many guys with whom I was doing time alongside were caught up in the same things, so much so that their goal was to bring what they no longer had to prison: drugs, sex, money and freedom. The drugs, sex and money temporarily freed them from the reality of their situation.

The problem was they neglected what they had. They had a mind, intelligence, good health and a multitude of other things. Fortunately, some of us saw what became of guys who were caught up in retrieving what they no longer had. Many of them never have and never will get their freedom. To make matters worse they either lost what they did have or it became severely retarded. Their minds, health, emotions, etc. were lost.

I went through a terrible depression. I was ready to

throw in the towel like many of my cohorts, chasing what was in the past, and worrying about what I didn't have. After seeing the reality of my situation and the situation of those around me I began to understand that it wouldn't do me any good fretting about anything other than what I did have.

Life Lesson

What my initial prison experience taught me is that in life there will always be things you don't have and things you do have. In prison, we go without many things that, prior to prison, seemed like necessities. Privacy, touch, heat, fire and sometimes hot water are things we go without. You can use what you got to get the things that aren't in your possession. Despite being without what can be considered necessities, convicts come up with ingenious ideas to replace or obtain what they don't have. I remember learning how to make a "stinger" to get hot water, popping a socket using pencil lead and toilet paper to get fire, and using a metal surface, batteries and a broken razor blade to light cigarettes. I watched in amazement as tattoo ink was created using soot from melted chess pieces and blue magic hair grease. What I witnessed in prison was a testament to getting what you want/need using what you have.

While I sat in prison, I did what I knew how to do to make the things I did have better. I worked on my emotions, my mind, my body, and whatever else I could think to work. I learned that what we have are tools. By sharpening our tools, we will be better equipped to get what we want but currently don't have.

People everywhere – whether in prison or in the lap of luxury – worry about what they don't have? Some of my peers in and out of prison failed to sharpen their tools and fell deeper and deeper into the bowels of prison. I focused on what I did have and used my tools to climb toward freedom. When I am eventually free, I will use my tools to flourish and get what I need and want.

Knowing that you have properly focused on what you have makes you confident that you will be able to get the things you currently are without. The need to worry about what you don't have becomes non-existent because you know your tools are sharp enough to eventually get it.

Summary

Focus on your tools because they are what you use to accomplish and obtain.

Action

1. Take inventory

Determine what tools you have at your disposal that will help you get what you want and need out of life.

2. Use your inventory

Sharpen the tools that you have and begin using them to get the things you want out of life and the things that you need. A confidence man (con man) will use his charm, intellect, gift of gab and knowledge of people to put a con over on a victim. He used his tools to get what he wanted: a victim.

***

I Learned From a Guy Billing Himself as the Roughest, Toughest, Realest Convict You'll Ever Meet That...

Pressure Bursts Pipes, No Matter Who They Belong To

I've seen people under various types of pressure, peer pressure; cultural pressure; pressure from isolation and many other types of pressure, burst.

Some people burst and give way to the prison culture. Others burst and give way to insanity. At one point during my stay at the Marion County Jail I was so tired of living in that environment, going back and forth to court and the threat of getting the maximum sentence I could no longer take it, I burst and signed a few plea bargains.

Our pipes burst when we go against what we believe, our principles or what we resolved to do because of a constant or persistent outside force.

Life Lesson

I was in the joint with this guy who was on his last leg of a 40-year sentence. This guy was billing himself as the roughest, toughest, realest convict you'll ever meet. He was cut-up and built like an action figure, bold and slick talking. His family name rang out in the city's streets and was reputable. He was involved in trafficking, assaults, intimidation, and affairs with staff while in prison.

His pipe burst when he was suspected of and questioned about his involvement with a staff member at the re-entry facility we were in. After several minutes of interrogation and threats, he basically slung himself and his mistress under the bus. He signed a note written by the lieutenant that questioned him. The note basically said the events, as the prison saw them, were true. I suppose he couldn't handle the pressure of being sent back to a real prison. He was put on the first thing smoking as soon as he signed that note despite being made promises – promises that would have allowed him to stay if they were honored.

This story has played out the same way over and over and over again my entire time in prison. A punk and a goon will give in eventually to the right amount and type of pressure.

Everyone has a point at which they will break.

I don't care if you are a trained special force operative or a devout monk you have a limit, so does the guy next to you.

I have learned that in order to keep from being broken or harmed by someone else being broke you have to know your limit and realize that others have a limit too.

I don't venture into endeavors that have

consequences I can't stand. Likewise I don't do anything with anyone who can't stand the consequences either.

Summary

Know your tolerances and the tolerances of those around you and stay below them.

Action

1. If you can't stand it… stay seated

We have or will have the opportunity to do things that have consequences we cannot stand to endure. If you don't know that you can handle those consequences don't get involved, stay out of the way.

2. Go it alone

If you are certain you can stand the consequences of the endeavors you undertake, go for it. However, if the penalties are severe, rest assured that if you take someone along and they end up having to face those penalties, they will fold. When they fold, they will fold back on to you. If the mission has the potential to get ugly, you better tackle it by yourself.

***

The Small World of Prison Taught Me That...

You Have a Purpose

I suppose one good thing that can be said about living in a maximum security prison is that you get time to think and make sense of things. I sat many years in a cell trying to understand what in the world was going on, and I never figured it out. However, I did come to realize that we are all here for some reason.

I don't think I have done anything in my life that is significant. I haven't invented anything, made millions, or found a cure. I've lived a non-unique life. Despite it all, I have lived through dozens of situations that I shouldn't have. I have survived multiple shootings, robberies, home invasions, drug deals, drug use, kidnappings and beefs. I even survived what the State of Indiana threw at me.

Sitting in a cell battling myself, I began to wonder why we are here. Eventually I began wondering why I am still here. I haven't contributed anything of value to mankind, and I have been nearly killed – physically and mentally – several times. Why am I still here?

Life Lesson

I don't think I've found the answer to my question. However, I know I am here to do something. Why else am I still alive and healthy, both physically and somewhat mentally? What my purpose is may very well be more modest than curing cancer or making millions of dollars, but it is a purpose nevertheless. I may just be here to positively impact one person's life.

Everything has been created for some purpose; not one of us is an exception.

Prison is a small world where you can see and experience nearly every aspect of it. Everything in that small world, similar to the real world, has its role, place and purpose. As a part of these worlds, I realized that I have a purpose, that we all have a purpose. Prison afforded me the chance to look back on the time I was shot. I just got out of a stalemate fighting hold with a guy when another person walked up beside me and shot me in my arm, breaking it instantly. He shot me in my stomach, too. I stumbled back not knowing I was shot from empirical evidence but from instinct. Burgundy blood was gushing down my arm and the front of my pants, looking like I pissed myself with blood. I immediately felt sleepy, and everything was dreamlike as the guy stood a few feet away with a pistol pointed at my face and unloaded the remainder of the clip, alternating his aim from my head to my feet. Despite his close proximity, caliber of the gun, and my playing with fire in the streets, I only suffered a graze in the neck. I must be here for some reason.

Prison can teach you that you have a purpose. Most likely your purpose is to serve someone else's purpose. Because many of us don't know what our purpose is or that we even have one, we are used by someone who realizes both their own purpose and ours (as it relates to theirs). Criminal justice agents realize that we are the oil and cogs that keep their employment opportunities rolling; for many years, that was and unfortunately still is my purpose. Your employer realizes that your purpose is to bring his vision to life, so he hires you.

Summary

Realize you have a purpose, find it, and fulfill it!

Action

1. Keep your skills sharp

We are all here to do something. We may not know what that something is, but until we figure it out we need to keep our skills sharp. Whatever our purpose, it will require some set of skills to complete. If our skills are already prepared, our purpose will more likely be fulfilled.

2. When it is time to go, go!

Until we figure out what we are here to do, those who understand their reason for living will utilize us to accomplish their goal. Once we figure out our purpose we can't be scared to fulfill it. We have to jump in and use those sharpened skills for our own purpose and not be afraid. If we don't go our chance for fulfillment may pass us by due to fear and inaction.

***

I Learned From an Old Man Who Sagged His Pants and Talked About Getting Out of Prison to Sell Dope and Buy Some 20-Inch Rims That…

Some Things Need to be Let Go

Many people mistakenly think prison is a place where criminals are rehabilitated. In reality, the likelihood of someone being rehabilitated in prison is very slim. The same crimes we commit to come to prison we have the opportunity and encouragement to commit while in prison. Battery, murder, rape, robbery, drug trafficking, etc. is a part of the prison culture.

Unfortunately, everybody or nearly everybody is or has been involved in crime while in prison; as if no one changes (for the better). The masses are still thinking, talking and acting the same despite growing older. People in the free world aren't too different: They get stuck and continue with what is familiar to them, even if it doesn't work.

I had the opportunity to see up close the insanity of not letting go of things that should have been, ages ago.

Life Lesson

Being witness to people holding on to things that made up their yesterday will teach you a few things. One important thing I have learned is to just let things go.

I used to sag, rob, smoke, drink, trap and all those things. However, I got older and realized all those things were senseless and part of my youth. As I matured, my values changed. On top of that, I wasn't in a situation to continue that behavior, and I wanted something new. As a result of this shift, I began to think differently, talk differently, and act differently.

On the other hand, some people in the joint were holding on to the past for dear life. One of my peers, who was 21 years into a 40-plus year sentence, talked about how he was going to get an old school Cadillac, put it on some rims, cop some dope from the connect, and take off. I really knew he had attachment issues by his hair style. If he was to wear a hat, it would appear that he had a head full of thick well-maintained Nubian locks, commonly referred to as dreadlocks. In reality, however, he was bald on top with locks growing thick around the sides and back of his head. If he can't let go and cut his hair bald, you know he won't let go of anything; he is probably a hoarder. The Bible talks about a person who can't let go of his riches. It says something along the lines of it being easier to get a camel through the head of a needle than it would to get a rich man in heaven. The rich man can't let go of his lifestyle, not even for a seat in heaven.

In addition to letting go of the things we used to do, we have to let go of our hang-ups and hate. I harbored hate for the guys who played a role in me being sent to prison and it was eating me alive. After a couple of years in prison, I realized I was only hurting myself by holding on. I was focusing on how I would get revenge on them and what the day would be like. I was going through the motions of handling my business so I could come home but my heart was turning black because it was submerged in plotting revenge. I look at hanging on to grudges and some things of the past like holding on to the hull of a sinking ship. If you don't let go you will eventually drown.

Summary

If your hands are full of garbage, you can't grab hold of the jewels life has for you, let go!

Action

1. Look at where you have been and where you want to go.

Your past will tell you why you aren't where you want to be. For example, when I look back at my life, I understand that my previous thinking and value system is the reason I am nowhere near where I want or need to be. I have an idea of where I want to be in life as well as where I need to be. That idea coupled with me looking back at my past allows me to determine some of the things that have kept me from my desired and required future.

2. Jettison everything that is keeping you from where you want to be

This is a very hard task. However, if you set your goal to get rid of everything that is barrier to your desired future you will likely rid your life of most of those barriers. Getting rid of barriers that are keeping you from where you want to be is like walking through a metal detector. In order to get through the detector you need take off your belt, rings, and any other thing that will make the detector go off. Take off the metal and get to where you want to be in life.

***

The Attacks on Our Minds in Prison Helped Me Learn That...

The Mind is Plastic, Fragile and Resilient

Prison is a dangerous place. Most people focus on guarding their physical safety. My focus eventually shifted to protecting my mind. I figured that everyone will eventually lose their life and you will have a hard time stopping someone who is determined from killing you. However, not everyone will lose their mind, especially if they protect it. The mind can be shaped, formed and molded. The things we consume, like information, ideas and images make up part of that molding process. Our minds are also fragile. It can come undone and give under pressure. The level of fragility varies from person to person. In addition, the mind can withstand some extreme conditions, and it can bounce back.

Prisons offer up many opportunities for the mind to be shaped, broken and redeemed. You are bombarded with all types of ideas, images and information. Most of the information is shocking, way out, and incorrect. You are constantly hit with conditions that will eventually drive you insane if you are not careful. These things present the mind with chances to demonstrate how weak or tough it is.

Life Lesson

In prison, I realized that the mind is plastic, fragile and resilient. Not only was I witnessing the attacks on the mind and it defending itself, I was experiencing it.

I have seen people completely transform themselves

by developing their minds. They limited many things that were negative and consumed as many things as possible that contributed to the positive shaping of their minds. I have seen one guy go from gun toting, grenade selling, killer who will never leave prison to a disciplined, intellectual teacher who is very humble and a great example of the mind bouncing back. I also have seen the opposite: good guys outside of prison turn to demons inside of prison.

A few guys I began my sentence with and knew from the street broke under the pressure constantly applied by maximum security prison. Some are undiagnosed loonies, others are diagnosed and doing the Thorazine shuffle. Back in the day, DOC would give inmates a drug called Thorazine that would make them all-the-way docile. They would drool on themselves and shuffle around aimlessly in short choppy steps.

Personally, there were several times I didn't think I was going to make it mentally. My mind, like those of my peers, was bombarded with all sorts of tortures. On top of our situation consisting of confinement, deprivation, starvation etc., we have to deal with deaths, rejection and the unexpected. I watched a man nearly break when he found out his 11-year-old daughter had sex with a boy and was now being called a slut at school. There wasn't a thing he could do to make the situation right. We sit in prison powerless. There wasn't a thing I could do sitting in prison about my cousin being murdered or my about my grandfather passing away. At times, I wanted to give up and let my mind go into an "I don't give a care" mode because dealing with the situation was becoming too much. However, I held on protecting my mind and consuming things that will at least begin to shape it into the right form.

Summary

Protect and strengthen your mind, it is impressionable and delicate but capable of rebounding.

Action

1. Do what you normally don't

We have a tendency to find a comfort zone and stay there, never venturing out unless forced. The problem with comfort zones is that it doesn't offer too many opportunities to learn. Doing new things strengthens the mind, forces it to learn. A mind that is strong and has a wealth of knowledge is more likely to withstand life's mental assaults.

2. Continue to learn, learn at least three things a day.

I had an instructor who would tell us that we had to learn three things a day about computers to keep our knowledge base relevant and up-to-date. This minimum applies to life as well. There are so many things in this world to learn and our brain is a sponge. We can use all there is to learn in the world to build up our minds, three things at a time.

***

A Kid From a City Up North that I Fought with Taught Me…

Don't Take Things Personal

Often we take things as an attack on us. Anytime someone criticizes what we say, what we do or what we think, we assume it is a hostile attack against who we are. I know dudes with whom you couldn't be a dissenting voice of any kind without them believing you are setting upon them with some violent force – a force that is a direct assault against their intellect, their manhood and their momma. Imagine nearly being stabbed with a makeshift prison knife because you told a Jerry Springer fan that Jerry Springer is a stupid show.

I've seen some extreme and not so extreme instances of things being taken personal. Those times when we catch an attitude or our feelings are hurt by a comment that was simply stated to express an opinion or thought are examples of taking things personal in a not so extreme manner.

Life Lesson

I had been locked up for over a year and was in a prison called the Reception and Diagnostic Center (RDC), being broken in before going to my final prison destination. At this facility, you spend most of your days testing or locked in a cell. This is your second stop on the way to prison. They fingerprint you, take your DNA, test your education level, do a health screening, do psychological testing, assign you a number, strip you of your individuality, and ultimately determine what facility you will end up in. During my testing, I was locked in a cell with another kid (we were both kids back then) who was from a city up north. He kept bashing the city I was from, but not in an overtly hostile manner. Before you are sent off to prison, you will be indoctrinated with some idea about beefing with other cities. This is especially true if you are in the county with someone who is in or has been to the joint before. No matter if you adhere to the indoctrination or not, it will always be on the back of your mind. Replaying what I was told about how dudes from other Indiana cities hate guys from Indianapolis, I began taking this kid's attacks personally, as if it was a direct attack against me. Then he said something about my favorite rapper; I took that personally, too. Long story short, we ended up fighting.

With this incident and many others, I had an epiphany: None of those people really or truly knew me and therefore weren't equipped to attack me personally. Because they weren't equipped, I shouldn't have taken what they said personally. Until I had that epiphany, I was tripping off nearly everything and was living in misery and getting into unnecessary trouble.

I learned that not everyone is attacking you when they criticize or disagree. I also began to understand others' points of view better and I stopped trippin' and getting in trouble. I am no longer miserable and thinking I am under constant attack. In addition I understand that I am not so important that everyone around me is lobbing personal attacks against my manhood.

You must have humility to not take things personally, especially living in an environment where you are spoken to and treated like a second-class lodger. However, humility, peace of mind and plain peace are very valuable. They are of greater value than protection from non-existent attacks, no matter what environment you are in.

I no longer take things personally, very often; instead I take things as assistance. Assistance in helping me become a better person: more humble; more discerning; more rational and more peaceful.

Summary

Don't take it personal, take it professional!

Taking it personal leads to emotional damage. Taking it professional means taking whatever you might take personal and using it to make you a better you.

Action

1. Determine if criticism is to hurt or help

Some people offer us constructive criticism designed to help us improve. Others offer it to hurt you. In Toastmasters, there is an evaluator who assesses the speakers to give them praise and constructive criticism in an attempt to help the speakers become better. In life, people offer us criticism to hurt our feelings and/or to embarrass us.

2. Use it or lose it

If the criticism is to help then use it. On the other hand, if it is to hurt use it as well but lose the source of the hurt. If people want to hurt you get rid of them. In the meantime, make the most of their attempts to hurt. Taking it personal leads to emotional damage. Taking it professional means taking whatever you might take personal and using it to make you a better you.

***

I Learned from Shorty Lott about the…

Power of Laughter

An emotion is expressed when we laugh. Usually, laughter is how we express a feeling of joy, sometimes a contemptuous joy. Any time you get to express how you feel, your emotions, it is therapeutic.

I met a guy in prison named Shorty Lott. He was about five-two and stocky with a flat top he converted to French braids. He had the coolest walk; it reminded me of those old school players catting down the avenue with his stable in tow. Still,

Shorty had the loudest, most annoying laugh I've ever encountered, which distinguished him from every convict in the prison. It didn't matter where he was in the dorm or where I was, I could always hear his distinguishable laugh. When I first met him, he was a few years into his bid with over 20 more actual years to go. Despite his situation, he was still able to laugh. Laughter was his therapy, and I never saw him mad or down trodden I only saw him in the best of spirits.

Shorty expressed his happiness through laughter and he expressed his realization of the absurdity in things said and done via his laughter.

Life Lesson

I continued to live my life even though I was in prison. I experienced things that made me happy, things that were funny, things that were extremely absurd and things that upset me. I was living in a place where many men lost touch with reality and themselves. From watching Shorty Lott, I learned that laughter kept him in touch with both. I took a page from his book and introduced into my life more and louder laughter. I not only laughed at all the things that were funny, I laughed when I was happy, when I realized an absurdity, and even when I was upset. I discovered how powerful laughter is. Laughing has kept me sane and plays a role in my perspective and my responses. For example, a guy who had been down for over 25 years when I met him said he couldn't believe that in the year 2000-and-something that we (Black men) were still coming to prison. It seemed that at that moment I saw how nonsensical my situation was; I couldn't do anything but laugh at it and myself for falling into the prison trap. There was no need to be upset or go crazy over it because the entire country knows better than to come to prison. Not to mention history and the language in the 13th Amendment every Black man should really know better than to end up in a cell.

Laughter has been powerful enough to help me stay

sane, alive and in touch. Some people may think I am crazy when I seem to be laughing at the thin air, however, there is so much that goes on around us... how can we keep from laughing? The crazy ones are those who can't, won't and don't laugh.

Summary

Find reasons to laugh and sanity, pleasure and reality will find you or remain with you if it hasn't been lost.

Action

1. Laugh

Look for the funny, the absurd and the entertaining in things, this is an excuse to laugh. If you have a reason to laugh you will have less reasons to be angry or to cry. When I was shot I had a reason to laugh. I found it absurd that I got shot and funny that I didn't die. I can look back at the incident and die laughing at how goofy my attacker looked running off after he shot me or the look on the undercover police's face as I fled despite him having given me an order to freeze with another pistol in my face. Keep in mind he watched my entire shooting unfold only to show his face after I am nearly dead and to show it behind a gun, if that isn't too funny I don't know what is. It's as if life is one big comedian, so we might as well laugh.

2. Laugh some more

Don't let the joke be on you. Turn things around. The people involved in my shooting ultimately had me sent to prison and even attempted to pay someone to kill me. They thought that my prison sentence would be my death sentence. However, I am here stronger than ever. I turned things around and only have reasons to laugh as an expression of my joy and happiness.

***

Having to Grow up in Prison I Learned that…

Change Creates Opportunities

When I talk about change in this instance, I am not talking about that gradual change; that kind of change happens in a manner that is unnoticeable. One day you are 16 years old, slim and young then as if overnight you are 30, fat and old. I am talking about the change that comes abruptly, noticeably and forcibly. Monday morning you are free and have self-determination but by Monday night your freedom and self-determination are literally gone.

With gradual change you are just going along

almost unaware of what is occurring. You are playing it safe not taking any chances or noticing opportunities. With abrupt change, you must get on board and adjust immediately. This change gives you the opportunity to do something different and to grow.

Life Lesson

I came to prison at a fresh 21 and didn't leave until I was close to 40. I basically grew up in prison, became a man and came into my own. My brain and body completed its development in prison. I had no choice but to do many things I had not done before. I embraced the changed I faced, going from liberated and determining my course of action without being compelled to enslavement and having my course determined for me. I went from a young kid who was plumb dumb to an old man who is not completely dumb, just some dumb.

My embrace wasn't overnight nor did it take a gang of years. In the early months, I longed for the streets, and like my peers I tried to live as if I were still home. One day I began looking at those around me still doing the same old things they have always done. They weren't growing or developing. I realized I was doing the same thing. All of us were looking like clowns. We even had a saying when people began to grow and do different things, we would say: "You ain't been doing it." For example, when a guy finally decided to get his GED at 40 years old, we would say something like: "Dude, you ain't been going to school."

I began to see the flaw in not jumping on the opportunities created by change. I realized that change created opportunities. My dramatic change of circumstances allowed me to stop and think, get a couple of degrees, learn about computers, and discover that there is more to life than thuggin' in the hood and in prison. It's sad to say, but it might have been too late by the time I would have learned these things as a free man.

Now when I am faced with change, I immediately

begin to look for the opportunities and things that I can get involved in that I haven't before or wouldn't otherwise and will aid in my growth.

I like to think that I have grown up, made changes and taken advantage of my circumstances. I don't want to be like the guys who go to prison and stay the same becoming an old fool.

Summary

Resistance to change is futile. Embrace it, because it comes bearing gifts of opportunities.

Action

1. Embrace change
Nothing stays the same. Change is a definite process a natural process. Fighting it is a waste of time and energy.

2. Look for new opportunities
When change occurs, opportunities are created. Those opportunities may not be apparent, but they

are there. Your time and energy can be used to find that opportunity instead of to resist the change.

***

A Model Prisoner Taught Me...

What Rational Thinking Consists of

The thing I find strange is that though we live in a community, everyone is selfish and inconsiderate. This is strange because members of a community are supposed to look out for and help one another. Members of a community work together to achieve what the individual can't accomplish alone. However, many of us only think about ourselves and live life without any thoughtful concern for those around us. At the same time, we expect to be given consideration from those we denied it to. Where is the rationality in that?

To me, rational thinking is a mixture of doing what is in your best interest and having consideration for the interest of others. I believe everyone should do what is best for them; Self-preservation is instinctual. While you are doing what is best for you, keep in mind the interest of others, the community.

Rational thinkers find a sustainable way of living. Crime isn't sustainable or in the best interest of the person committing the crime. While the rational thinker is eating, he isn't stopping anyone else from eating. For example, a farmer who thinks rationally will work his land in a manner that feeds him and his family while not harming the environment or surrounding land. He knows his land will feed him and generations to come. In addition, he knows other farmers have to eat and feed their families as well.

Life Lesson

In prison you meet so many people who are selfish.

They don't care about anything or anyone as long as they get what they want. They are so shortsighted and selfish they don't care if they burn their bridges getting what they want in that moment. Those guys who get released on a sentence modification or some early release program and then commit another crime also are examples of irrational thinkers. They don't care about their long-term best interest or the interest of the community they are part of.

Early in my sentence, I met a dude who was given a long prison term for drugs. He was a model prisoner. He was very smart and got all sorts of degrees. A judge let him out 10-15 years early. He walked away a free man from a maximum security prison. He gets out and a few months later was sitting next to me in that same maximum security prison. Then this guy went out there and got caught up in a drug sting.

What he did was burn the bridge to freedom for himself and the prison community. He can never get out early again. Unfortunately many guys behind him, no matter how good they are or what they have accomplished in prison, will ever be released early.

You would think that people living in such a small micro-community like prison would consistently do what is best for themselves while not harming the rest of the group; however, the opposite is true. For many years I wondered why this was the truth. I came to conclude that it was due to a lack of rational thinking.

No one in their right mind would be out to get "theirs" while screwing over those in the group on the same mission. In addition, no one who is sane would jeopardize and/or ruin their interest or the interests of others for immediate and ephemeral gratification.

I was an irrational thinker (I still backslide into the world of irrationality from time to time). It is a shame I had to go to prison to learn about rational thinking.

Summary

Thinking with regard for your own interest while simultaneously having consideration for others' interest is rational thinking.

Action

1. Always look out for yourself

You have to take care of yourself. No one else will, and you shouldn't expect them to. If you don't have your things in order, you can be of no use to anyone else. To look out for someone else, you have to look out for yourself and put yourself in a position to be able to help.

2. Apply the Golden Rule

While you are in the process of looking out for yourself, do unto others as you would have them do unto you. You don't want your toes stepped on, so don't step on any toes. Just as you have to eat, so does the next person. Don't take the food from their mouths so you can get fat.

***

While at a Re-entry Facility I Learned…

Loyalty Lies in the Vice

People are steadfast in allegiance and faithful to their vice. Whatever a person's vice is, they are faithful to that vice and place it before people.

Vices are bad habits that contribute to a person's failure, shortcomings, degradation or immorality. I look at vices as things that people consume that contribute to their bad health; whether that health be mental, physical, emotional, financial, social or involving relationships.

People aren't loyal to each other, they are loyal to

vices. We can be married, but some of us won't be loyal to our spouses though we will be loyal to our vice known as lust. Having sex with anyone other than our spouse will surely be bad for the health of our marriage. Likewise, drug addicts (and dealers as well) don't care about their friends and family. However, they will go through hell and high water to get drugs and use drugs.

Life Lesson

I learned where loyalty lies sitting in prison observing and experiencing. In prison, at some point, all of us talk about how we are going to change, how we love our kids, our family, and our girl, how we are tired of the things we used to do and the way we used to live. However, as soon as we get access to whatever our vice is, we forget about all that change rhetoric we spoke about.

In prison, we bond with people and become good friends. We look out for each other and break bread with one another. That bond is always and easily broken over some vice. This became very clear to me when I was front row to several very similar incidents. The incident that most sticks out occurred at the last prison I was in. Toward the end of my bid, I went to a re-entry facility. We were given many privileges, and the facility was wide open compared to the other controlled movement high security prisons I was housed in. The entire state wanted to be transferred to this prison. Many people were shipped out of this facility and sent back to regular prisons for cell phones and drugs. Dudes were cutting deals with staff in order to stay after getting caught with phones and/or drugs. One guy was on his way back to a regular prison for being caught with porno movies, after getting caught with a phone previously. However, he cut a deal in order to stay. He had to give up a stash of phones, drugs or other contraband. He told the staff where his backup stash of dummy phones was located. Dudes kept these stashes for this purpose. When the staff went to retrieve the stash, it was gone. His buddy stole the stash before the staff got to it. The vice of drugs and money overrode friendship and loyalty. They knew this guy was going to get sent to a horrible prison with time added to his sentence, but they didn't care. They wanted to be loyal to their vice.

They were faithful to the vice and not the person. I know that anyone with a vice will, at some point, put that vice before me. The only way to get their loyalty is to be the vice or the gate keeper to it.

Summary

For the vice, a person will show his virtue in the form of loyalty.

Action

1. Limit your vices

The more vices you have, the more masters you have. Each vice gives something and someone control over you. Getting rid of vices gives you more control over your present and future.

2. Use the vice

Some vices just can't be shook. The ones that still remain after you have placed a limit on them should be utilized. You know how your vices make you react and make you think. You can use that knowledge to market and sell a product or service that caters to that reaction and way of thinking. All vices can be used for someone's benefit. Try to be the beneficiary of the vice – not the slave to it.

***

Finger Pointers Taught Me That...

You Can't Give Everybody Advice

People of all shapes, sizes and ages have experiences that allow them to give people advice. We may have been through what our peer is currently going through and can advise him or her on how to navigate through the situation.

One problem with giving advice arises when you are offering it to someone who isn't receptive or just flat out doesn't want to hear it. Some people have given me a piece of advice only to be met with an attitude, hostility and disrespect. I've experienced the same things as the giver of the advice. I was giving my little brother some advice about going back to school and must have rubbed him the wrong way or said something out of order: He got kind of hostile with me. His hostility was brief, but very apparent to me, and I kept the rest of my 2 cents to myself, and I still do.

Some people may say you won't have the above problems if you give advice when it is asked for. However, the fact is that you can't give advice to some people whether they ask or not.

Life Lesson

In the joint, we like to point fingers and blame everyone in the world – except ourselves – for our problems. I noticed what seemed to be a trend as it related to advice. We receive a lot of advice from each other, staff, lawyers, family, books, etc. However, when we take the advice and things don't turn out as expected, we blame the source of the advice.

From my own experience and watching nearly every convict I lived with, I learned that by blaming the advice giver we don't learn from our mistakes. In some cases, we don't realize we made a mistake, outside of taking the advice. Often the problem was our implementation of the advice not the advice itself.

The lesson is that some people shouldn't be given advice. Those who are always pointing fingers don't want advice. You may be doing them an injustice by giving them someone to blame as opposed to learning from the mistake they made. To me, the worst thing that can come from a mistake is not learning from it. Sometimes advice gives people a reason not to learn from their mistake. In the county jail as you wait the outcome of your case, you will receive advice to "box it up." That means you will be advised by your peers to take your case to trial as opposed to taking a plea bargain. Most followers of the advice run in the courtroom to face a jury and end up getting split to the white meat. Instead of looking at their lifestyle, the one that landed them in the position to have to worry about pleas and the jury box, they blame the advice. They feel as if they would be free if they hadn't taken the advice to "take it to the box."

Some people benefit more from either getting their head busted or reaching success on their own than they do from a helping hand. Experience is the best teacher because you are given the opportunity to learn and not blame. Look at us convicts and ex-cons – we had to go to prison before we learned something. All the advice from friends, family and society didn't teach us a thing. Instead, it only acted as fodder for our blame game and as an excuse not to engage in a learning process.

Summary

You can't cast your advice before all; to some, it may be more harmful than helpful.

Action

1. Let them come

Don't force feed anyone anything, especially advice. Let them seek it out. If you offer unsolicited advice, it won't be appreciated or digested properly.

2. Be open and ready

Be willing to give advice so when people are ready to humble themselves and seek advice out they know they can come to you.

***

**Something My Momma Told Me After I
Was Sentenced Taught Me That...**

It Takes a Real Situation to Get to Know a Person for Real

A real situation is one where we are tested and pushed to a point where it is either hold up or fold up. A real situation is what many criminals find themselves in when they get caught. The law has their foot on the criminals' necks, applying so much pressure that many fold up and tell on themselves, their partners and anyone else they are asked to.

A real situation is one where your character is exposed, and it's either put up or shut up. What are you going to do under peer pressure or when you think no one is looking? What are you going to do when that situation you never thought would come, does? Are you going to follow through with all that stuff you were talking about?

For me, my real situation lasted over a decade and it was called prison. Prison allowed me to get to know people for real.

Life Lesson

Prior to my prison situation I thought everyone in my circle was real, and I was swearing up and down I knew them. However, I was fortunate enough to find out that I never truly knew anyone in my circle.

All except one of my so-called friends pretty much washed their hands of me; many of my relatives did the same. Surprisingly, that was the best thing they did: I got to learn more about them. Some of my friends joined forces with the people who played a role in me being sent to prison, others ran off with money, and some even tried to slander me. Their character was exposed, and despite what they said they would do, they folded.

Parts of my family have been there from day one going above and beyond what I ever expected from them. I got an opportunity to see them in a real situation. When I was sentenced my momma told me something I will never forget. We were on the phone, and she said: "Lamar!" (that's my middle name) "Your friends won't be there for you, and I am not back there with you..." meaning she wasn't in Indiana. She went on to say: "...but I am going to do everything I can to help you." That is exactly what she did.

Not only did I get to know my friends, family and relatives, I got to know my prison cohorts as well. Even though I lived with them in prison in the same cell house and even in the same cell, I really didn't get to know them until they were placed in one of those real situations. As a result of those situations, I found out many of the guys I were friends with were in the closet homosexuals, working with the police, couldn't be trusted, and succumbed easily to vices at the expense of their friends. Some stood tall through it all.

If these guys weren't placed in situations where their character was tested, I would have never known who they really were. I doubt that you know who your friends and family really are if they haven't been tested, pushed and placed in a character exposing circumstance. I am not talking about a circumstance that tests your strength; I am talking about the ones that test your weakness.

Summary

It's easy to be real when it's all good but you get to find out who is who when it is all bad.

Action

1. Take an inventory of yourself and your friends

Sometimes an honest look will show that you may or may not be who you and other people think you are. It may also show that others are more than you think.

2. Look for these five things:

i. Is the person responsible?

ii. Is the person accountable?

iii. Do they know how to prioritize?

iv. Are they a self-advocate?

v. Do they engage in the above four things with respect?

***

I Learned From Knocking Out My Prison Sentence That...

A Lot Can be Accomplished One Step at a Time

When we have a task ahead of us that appears like it will take forever to accomplish, many of us give up. Likewise, if the task seems like it will be extremely difficult, we have a tendency to abort.

The only way to finish a difficult and time consuming endeavor is to actually start it and see it through to completion. To think a challenging task should be completed overnight is a mistake and so is giving up when it isn't accomplished instantaneously. I realize we live in a fast food, high-speed Internet and instant message society, so we want results immediately, however, we shouldn't move on leaving our task incomplete because the results don't appear promptly.

There exists a failure to understand that if we work toward something in small incremental steps we can achieve great things and many things. Attempting to conquer the world in one swoop will lead to failure. However, the likelihood of achieving world domination is increased using small calculated steps.

Imagine a boxer getting in the ring, and every punch he throws is a power-packed potential knockout blow. His goal is to win the fight in the first round. When he doesn't land that first round KO, he is out of gas for the remaining rounds and basically throws in the towel. For the next 9 or 10 rounds, his opponent puts one foot in front of the other using his jab and combos and wins the fight. The former boxer wanted immediate results and learned the hard way about the value of taking one step at a time. Those small jabs and blows to the body that seemed futile early on began to hurt later in the fight and led to a victory for the later boxer.

Life Lesson

Going to prison with so much time and a long road ahead of me left me with no idea about what to do or how I was to do it. The reality was I had to do all those years one day at a time. When I began my sentence I only saw a never ending dark road. I just kept pushing forward hoping that I would somehow someday come through the darkness. I kept my head down while I pushed until I saw light shining on my shoe. The next thing I knew I was on my way home.

I had no choice but to learn that you can scale a mountain doing it one day and one step at a time. Before I learned it was true I had to believe that one step at a time gets things done was true. I couldn't give up or believe anything other than I was going to knock out my time in small steps. The only alternatives were to go crazy or to die.

Once I truly believed anything can be done using incremental paces many other tasks became less daunting and possible. Completing college and writing this book became simple.

Summary

Many small maneuvers can lead to one big achievement!

Action

1. Set a goal
If you have no idea where you want to go, you can end up and be led anywhere. Without a goal, you will often be led astray. You must have something to strive for.

2. Push your pawns
With your goal clearly outlined, begin to push your life's pawns in place until your goal is reached.

Pawns move one space at a time. They go unnoticed, because one step doesn't appear to be a power move. However, a multitude of single steps equates to a power move – a power move no one saw coming.

***

Footie Taught Me That...

People Will Say Anything

Some people will let anything fall out of their mouths. They seem to not have any sort of leash or filter on their tongues. People will tell you lies using fanciful hard to believe stories or smart hard not to believe ones. They will tell you all of their business and all of someone else's. People will disrespect you with uninhibited simplicity or with similar complexity and do it without being provoked. People will string together words to form sentences that make no sense and will use words that make no sense in a sentence.

Sometimes I find myself scared to talk to some people. I have no idea what they might say. To make matters worse I don't know what I might let fall out of my mouth in response. In addition, I fear I might fall for some fanciful lie or not go for an easy to believe truth.

I also feel embarrassed and ashamed as I attentively listen to a narrator telling all of his business and gossiping about someone else's business.

I pray when I have to talk to someone that they don't lob disrespect at me out of the blue.

I cringe when I hear people talk, and I can't understand them or when I can understand them despite using words that they shouldn't; for example, when people say "pacific" when they meant "specific." I cringe because I know I can sound the way they do to someone else.

If you listen close and pay attention you will begin to notice that people will say anything especially when they have a reason, some want your vote, your friendship, your money and insight.

Life Lesson

In the joint, you have all kinds of people crammed into very small spaces. All of these people have as many different things to say and probably even more going on in their minds. I don't know if I was fortunate or unfortunate for having heard some of the things these people had to say and having a peek into their minds via their mouths.

I can say I was fortunate to learn that people will say anything. Now I listen closely, ask questions or stop the nonsense before it gets started and out of hand.

The fact that people will say anything became clear to me in one incident. I was playing cards with a guy named Footie. Footie was a great storyteller and a liar. I learned the hard way that he would say anything, especially to get what he wanted. I let him talk me into loaning him some money (It was actually commissary, or food prisoners are allowed to buy.) so he could try to make some money gambling. I was on my way to school; he wasn't around, so I left a few dollars' worth of peanuts on my bed. I told him where they were and that he could grab them. When I returned from school, he tried to play me like he never got the money, however, the peanuts were nowhere to be found. He stuck to his story. No one else was petty enough to steal peanuts. He was willing to say anything for peanuts, literally.

I realized Footie would say anything. After that point, I began to notice that all people, free or not, will say anything. They will say things they don't believe – being politically correct, things they don't know anything about, crazy things, incoherent things, persuasive things and all sorts of things.

Having the ability to think critically comes in handy while listening to people talk. Likewise, knowing better comes in handy, like knowing better than to talk to this or that person.

Summary

If you believe anything and sometimes if you don't, people will tell you anything if you let them.

Action

1. Just listen

If you just listen to people talk, don't interrupt, don't criticize and don't judge they will likely tell you any and everything. If, however, you don't want to hear it…

2. Interrupt

The moment you cut someone off and let them know you know they are full of it, they will stop telling you any and everything. In fact, they won't tell anyone anything when you are around because they know you know they are lying and using hyperbole.

***

From Watching Kenny I Learned That
It's...

Not Over Until You Are Dead

Me and many others like me have been and continue to be sent to prison with crazy sentences. When my prison sentence was handed out, I felt as if I were dead. I couldn't wrap my head around a 20-year prison term let alone the 52 years I was originally given. What I faced was an event that left me feeling like life was over; this feeling only increased as my friends and relatives closed the casket on me. In other words, they treated me as if I were dead; however, they didn't bother to visit my gravesite. Some people lose body parts, loved ones, or their careers and have similar feelings to the ones I did.

When people begin to believe that their lives are over, they start doing things that make their situation worse. For example, some people become apathetic toward life, commit suicide or murder. They failed to understand that as long as we are alive we can improve our situation and overcome our individual event that leaves us feeling like it is all over. If we are alive, we can still solve problems, ask for and receive help, and we can get lucky.

On the other hand, if we are dead there isn't a thing we can do. A dead person can't solve his problem, can't offer or ask for help and he surely can't get lucky. There isn't a thing a dead person can do to turn his situation around.

Life Lesson

In a prison where most of the population will be in there for decades or forever, there is a widespread feeling of life being over, so people making their situation worse is the norm. They engage in risky behavior that jeopardizes their safety and health; they adopt an "I don't give a care" attitude, they commit suicide and murder. All these behaviors eventually lead to death, and when you are dead that's when it is over.

How I came to truly learn that life wasn't over as a result of my sentence was by watching what wasn't considered the norm: People who aren't slowly or rapidly throwing away their lives. They haven't given up and stuck it out.

To be honest, many of the guys I watched had, at one point, given up and adopted an apathetic attitude and were involved in risky behaviors. However, they survived and had an epiphany. Their survival of a bad situation made worse by their attitude and actions made them realize that their lives weren't done as long as they were still kicking. Some kept fighting and working hard and won their freedom and some worked as an example and a testament to the fact that life goes on. I credit these guys with motivating me to keep pushing and helping me realize that my life was not over. Some of the ones who won their freedom are successful and further prove that life isn't over until you are gone. I was in prison with a guy named Kenny. Kenny had done about 27 straight years in prison by the time I come across him. However, he never stopped fighting and eventually won his freedom. Unfortunately, he died about four months later. Nevertheless, he was able to get out of prison because he was alive.

My fellow convicts showed me how to wrap my head around my sentence. Then they showed me how to continue to live. Here I am today after 14 years in prison living. As long as I am alive anything is possible even if I fall I can eventually bounce back.

Summary

Life, not death, offers us the opportunity and

resources to improve ourselves and our situation no matter how bad we are or how bad it is.

Action

1. Come to terms
Whatever situation you are in accept it because it is reality. Ignoring it or denying it isn't going to help you improve your circumstances.

2. Get up
As long as you are alive you have the ability to get up and do something about your circumstances. No matter what barriers are in place, what obstacles you come across or how many doors shut in your face if your heart is beating you climb over barriers, run through obstacles and kick down doors. Kenny kicked down the doors to prison; it took him a while, but he did it.

***

While I Sat in Prison, My Family Helped Me Realize That...

You Must Have Something Greater Than Reality

Reality is whatever we are living through or whatever our situation is. I believe that we should never be content with or defeated by our reality; as a result of that belief, I know we need to strive for something that transcends what we are currently living through. This thing that transcends can be a person, place, thing, idea or whatever works for you. In essence it becomes a goal that you strive to achieve while giving you hope.

No matter who we are, we have a reality. We are living through one thing or another. We can have a nine to five job, a happy or bad marriage, or even be living like a king or baron. My reality was living in prison slightly above an animal, now it is living as a social pariah.

The good thing is that having something greater than my reality is easy, simply because I am on the lowest rung of society and near the lowest point of my life. For others, finding something that acts as a goal, as motivation or as hope may be difficult. Some people are on the highest rung of society and have accomplished and collected so much that there is nothing left to do. However, there is always something that is greater than what was and what is, and we need to have that something – whether it is the kingdom of God or exploration of outer space. That thing will work to keep you moving toward something better and keep you motivated when you may have given up otherwise.

Life Lesson

I learned that I needed something greater than my reality relatively quick after I found myself in prison. When I first arrived at the maximum security prison I had no idea what to do or what I was going to do. I was deeply depressed and my spirit was depleted. At that point, I was vulnerable and could have easily fallen head first into the prison culture.

The one thing that kept me motivated and gave me hope was my family, specifically those family members investing their time, money and trust in me. They were greater than that situation. My goal became to return home to them as soon as I could. They gave me hope. As long as they were there with me, I believed I would be there with them soon.

I also knew I had talents that would allow me to create a future many times better than my present and past. I clung to my family and my abilities and kept from becoming institutionalized. I was motivated to stay away from the drugs, the violence, and the nonsense. I knew that if I extended my stay in prison or didn't come home, I would let my family down and would be further wasting my capabilities.

Many people in situations similar to mine give in to their current reality and are defeated by it. They come to believe they are in the situation they are destined to be in, and complacency sets in. People in prison say "forget it" and go all in; that is, they make prison their home and give up on life outside of the fence or wall. They get a knife, a boy (homosexual), a mule, some dope and a TV. They get swept away in the prison nonsense until they become institutionalized. They have nothing that is greater than their reality. There was a guy I used to hang with named Paul. Paul had around 52 years. He was standing strong, going to school and going hard in the gym. Next thing I knew he had given up. He destroyed all of his paper work (documents vital for fighting your case), dropped out of college, started having sex with other men, and ended up nearly beating a correctional officer to death. He had nothing greater than his reality.

Watching people go all in made me realize I had to have something greater.

Summary

You have to see past what it was and what it currently is and move toward that line of sight that allows you to see and have what is greater.

Action

1. Don't settle

If your current reality isn't the greatest it can be, don't sit there content. I believe that what we can achieve is limitless. No matter how successful we are in our current reality, we always can be and do greater.

2. Define and persist

Outline what you want your greater reality to look like and then take constant and consistent steps toward that desired reality. Once that reality is reached, define and work toward an even greater one. While in prison, many people outline a reality that consists of freedom. When they obtain that freedom they move on to greater things. In fact, they map out various levels of realities one being better than the next. Then they constantly reach each level.

***

A Pair of Brothers Let Me Know That...

There are No Excuses

Everyone engages in some sort of task. Everyone wants to have some sort of lot in life. At some point, everyone will fail at a task, at acquiring that desired lot, and will fail period. Most people will blame their failures on a multitude of things. They will blame others, circumstance and anything else they can think of. They come up with all sorts of excuses as to why they failed. I have learned that there aren't any excuses.

In prison, resources are limited at best and often

non-existent. Despite the resource issues prisoners still must carry out and accomplish their desired tasks. Depending on how much they bit off failure to get the task done can mean bodily harm or death. No excuse can be valid enough to justify the task not getting done. Your word is one of the most valuable currencies in prison. Convicts have become good at making something out of nothing because they have to and excuses won't put food in your belly, money in your pocket nor will it keep the goons off your back. Real convicts don't make excuses, they make it happen.

I had a cousin in prison who could get just about anything in there. He made it happen; he didn't make excuses. He was so successful he told me he liked prison more than he does the streets. Like a true convict, instead of making excuses he made solutions. Solving problems is what improves one's lot and gets the tasks done.

Life Lesson

No one wants to hear excuses, so to me they don't exist. I used to believe in excuses. After being in prison and being forced to come up with solutions to problems caused by a lack of resources and watching my peers come up with ingenious solutions my belief in excuses waned.

What really made me realize that there are no excuses was a pair of brothers I met in prison. Despite not having any support from the streets they got along in prison pretty well. Their situation reminded me of people in or from underdeveloped countries who change the world without having all the amenities and resources of a person from a developed nation. The brothers came up with solutions and disregarded the excuses.

I can't recall these brothers making excuses or crying about their situation; they just went on about their business. One of these brothers said something to me that really hit home and made me realize I had no excuse to be involved in any nonsense or crying while in prison. I had family support; they didn't. Despite being on their own, they didn't cry or make excuses. I asked one of them if he was going to send his mother a Mother's Day card, he said, "I would if I knew where she was at." His words pierced my heart because I couldn't imagine not having my momma in my life and not crying and playing the blame game. They never cried or blamed her for a thing.

Looking at them making it I came to understand that excuses are irrelevant and useless. Without outside support and with scarce prison resources these brothers got along and thrived in prison without blaming and crying just solving the problems they faced.

Summary

There aren't any excuses, unless you excuse yourself to find a solution!

Action

1. Excuse yourself

Before you even think about making an excuse remove yourself from the situation the room or wherever you are so you can think. Go somewhere where you can think clearly of a solution.

2. Return

After you have excused yourself and thought of a solution to replace an excuse, come back to the situation or the room. You don't necessarily need to return with the cure for cancer, just an idea, a suggestion, or anything that can help spark idea creation in others or a brainstorming session as opposed to an excuse conference.

***

My Cousin Taught Me That…

Lust is Thicker Than Blood

When I was a kid, I would get lessons in brotherly
love. Any time I would choose my friends over my
brother, my momma would tell me that blood is
thicker than water. At the time, I had no idea what
she was talking about. I eventually came to
understand that blood represented family and water
symbolized non-family; blood is thicker, meaning
that family will be around long after my friendships
dried up.

What I have come to learn, while in prison, is that

there is a substance seemingly thicker than blood. That substance is lust. It isn't thicker in a sense that it will be around long after the blood disappears. It is thicker in that men and women alike will place their sex partner or potential partner before their family. Blood in this case still represents family and lust represents that person we are having sex with. That feeling of ecstasy provided by that partner seems to be more powerful than anything provided by family.

Life Lesson

Since I have been in prison I have experienced the thickness of lust first hand and as an observer. When I started my sentence, I was put on the back burner for lust. I had a cousin who would come to see me. Then one day she stopped coming and writing. I couldn't figure out why all contact had stopped. I found out that her boyfriend was locked up as well. She was going to see him and doing things for him that she would never have done for me; all this for lust and none of it for blood.

I have seen dude's sisters and mothers come to see their boyfriends and not their brothers or sons despite them being in the same prison.

On a positive note, I have had women put me before their family and do things for me they wouldn't do for their brother or cousin. It is sad that I can count on someone I'm not related to but can't count on too many people I share blood with.

What really solidified this lesson was the story of one of my peers. He was in prison for retaliating against his sister's boyfriend for assaulting his sister. In the end, the sister sided with her abusive boyfriend. Now the brother is in prison while the sister is lying in the arms of her violent beau.

I can't explain why lust is thicker than blood, but it has been my experience that it truly is.

Summary

Blood is thick, just not thick enough!

Action

1. Don't mix the two

Don't pit your family against you lover and don't pit yourself against your family's lover. If you are having issues with your lover, don't call a family member to resolve it, especially if you know it can get out of hand and if you know you will be right back with you lover next week. Likewise, don't meddle in your family's domestic affairs if you know it can turn into a UFC match followed by a scene from "Gangsters in the Hood" ending with the lovers back together.

2. Don't bet on it

If you have to bet against lust and you are riding with blood, you are making a mistake. There may be a time when blood wins, but more often than not lust will be the victor. Just know that lust is a formidable adversary not to be taken lightly.

***

My Girlfriend, Who Got Pregnant by Another Man, Taught Me That…

People Have Their Own Lives to Live

When we are born, we are given a life to make due with. Until we become parents, all we really have to do is live that life. We aren't obligated to help anyone else live their life. Everyone living is given his own life to live, and we must keep that in mind.

Once we are born we are in the game of life. We are nurtured and taught so that we might play the game successfully. In other words, we are given tools that will, hopefully, allow us to live our own lives and be independent, interdependent at worst.

Those teaching and raising us know that each individual has his or her own path. They know that people are focused on their lives, playing their own game, and may not have the time or resources to help us through our portion of this game of life. As a result, they attempt to equip us with tools that allow us to live our lives, either independent of or interdependent with the lives of others.

We aren't raised to go through this game of life putting our lives on pause while helping someone else live his life; except parents. Once we have kids, our lives are supposed to come second to the lives of our children.

The mistake many of us make is expecting people to put their lives on hold for us. Then we get upset when people have the nerve to live their own lives and not ours. We are foolish enough to think our lives are more important to another than their own life is to them.

Life Lesson

When I was arrested, I had a girlfriend that I had been seeing for about eight months. She rode with me for a year while I sat in the county jail. When I left the county jail in 1999, my earliest possible release date was 2024. Somewhere during my year stay in the county jail, I got the idea that this girl was going to ride my sentence out with me. I expected her to put her life on hold and help me live mine.

Once I left the county and went off to prison, I never saw her again. She had moved on, and before I had time to unpack and move into my cell, I found out she was expecting a baby.

This girl, those I thought were my friends, and my relatives all kept it moving. After my anger subsided, I began to understand a fact: Everyone has a life to live.

I understand that we all have the right to pursue happiness. We all have to focus on making it through this world. I had to realize my situation and understand that life for my girlfriend, friends, and relatives went on. They still had to pay bills, deal with relationships, and work through the complexities of the world. They had to live their lives not live my life.

Once I reconciled that fact in my mind, I stopped being angry with those who chose to live their life. Now, I simply hope people have consideration and recognize it when they see me living my life. I don't have time, resources or the willingness to live anyone else's life but my own.

Summary

Live your life. Don't trip off those doing so, as everybody has their own life to work with and focus on.

Action

1. Live

You were given a life just like the next man, so live it. Your life will look different from everyone else's because you are different from everyone else. You have to make your own way and do what makes you happy.

2. Let live

Don't make someone else's life hard and miserable and don't live their life for them. The fact is that if you have the time to live someone else's life you can't be living your own. Leave people alone to focus on their lives while you do the same. After all, this life is about living.

***

From Drew I Learned That…

Life Isn't Fair

I remember, as I was growing up, my momma making sure that if I got something my brother did too, and vice versa. If he got two pieces of candy, she made sure I had no more than two pieces. She was basically teaching us about fairness. Via these lessons and others we learn in society, we begin to feel that life is or should be fair. Referees and judges attempt to make things fair. However the truth is life will never be fair despite referees, judges, parents and intervention.

People have different talents, capabilities, access to resources, knowledge bases, etc. These differences make life unfair. Is it fair that my friend is different physically, which allows him to run faster? Is it fair that a person with inferior capabilities has a contact that gets him a good job while I flip burgers?

Life is so dynamic and complex that it can't be limited by fairness.

Life Lesson

I was in the joint going to school, working, eating humble pie, and staying out of trouble. Every time I put something in court to get an early release, it would get shot down. Seeing guys who were always in trouble and doing wrong getting love in court was frustrating.

In 2005, I received my AS and BS. Despite my accomplishment, I couldn't get any love in court. When I saw a guy named Drew get some love in court, I truly began to understand that life just isn't fair. Drew had just got caught for his involvement with drugs. His EPRD went from around 2007 to 2018 as a result. All he pretty much did in prison was move and use drugs. The next thing I knew, he was on the bricks. The courts granted him a sentence modification and sent him home.

Drew wasn't the exception. Many of the people who were on BS in prison got love from the judge. I accepted the fact that life and every part of it was unfair. All I can do is ride the wave of unfairness when it favors me and endure it when it doesn't.

We all know that the Founding Fathers lied when they said all men were created equal. They weren't being sincere or truthful when they spoke about equality. The nature of life is unfair along with the byproducts of life. Knowing this gives us the chance to find ways to benefit from life's unfairness more often than being penalized for it.

I don't cry about how life is because I understand that's what it is. It's unfair. I just take care of my business and don't worry about the rest of it.

Summary

There is too much going on and too many opportunities in this life; it won't be limited by fairness.

Action

1. Don't cry

Life is unfair, so there is no need to cry about it. Crying isn't going to level the playing field. In fact, I believe it makes matters worse because you are wasting valuable resources whining, crying and complaining. Those resources can be put to better use by doing something to even the results. You might have to work harder than a mentally or physically gifted person, but you can still get the same results. Having to work harder may not be fair, but that's life, so don't cry.

2. Take advantage

Look for ways to utilize the unfairness created by

life. Someone noticed that some of us aren't mathematically inclined and so created a calculator. Someone noticed that some of us are physically weak and so created the pulley. Someone noticed that some of us are program language illiterate and created WordPress. Find ways to level the results of what happens on the playing field and you just might get rich; wouldn't that be unfair to a smart, physically superior poor person?

***

Due to the Actions of Correctional Officers, I Had to Learn…

He Who Cares Less Wins

When we are caught up and let our emotions get the best of us, we are at a disadvantage. In many situations, the person who doesn't care will come out on top.

Back when my brother and I were kids, I used to pick on him until he went crazy. The angrier he got, the more enjoyment I received. As long as he cared that I picked on him, I was the winner. If he ever stopped caring, I would cease to have fun, and he would be the winner.

Life Lesson

In prison, we become the little brothers.
Correctional officers pick with us and feed off our
anger and misery. I figured out that if I stop caring I
will be left alone. In addition, it makes life easier
especially when you are in prison. I stopped caring
about people and things in the streets; I couldn't do
anything about them anyway. When you don't care,
you can't be hurt. I learned to play poker in prison.
The only time I won was when I didn't care about
losing.

The ability and willingness to not care separates real
goons from busters. A goon doesn't care and is
willing to put everything on the line; a buster isn't,
and a real goon wins every time. A real goon goes
all in not caring if he wins or loses while a buster
folds or calls only to be worried about losing his
bet.

Once you exclude fear, anger and any other limiting
emotion, like attachment, you can deal better with

facts and reality. Dealing with facts helps you make better decisions.

Even though I beat the correctional officers by not caring and kept from going crazy by doing the same thing, it's hard to turn my caring switch back on. Now I am having trouble caring about people, their circumstances and other situations. I was told I am harsh and don't care about a thing. When they called me that, it didn't bother me.

Summary

If you care too much, those who don't will defeat you!

Action

1. Care enough not to

If you care at all or care too much, you may be doing yourself harm. People who care are usually enablers. I see this all the time in parents. They will take care of their grown kids allowing them to sleep all day and play video games all night. They refuse to allow them to be homeless and hungry while instead allowing them to be lazy and irresponsible. You have to not care about them being homeless and leave them in the streets, you have to not care about them being hungry and let their stomachs growl. If you allow them to sit in your house sleeping and gaming, they won't ever get on their feet. If you leave them in the rain, they will get off that behind and find a roof and some food; more importantly, they will acquire the skills needed to keep from going homeless and hungry. When you care, you are enabling them to be lazy and irresponsible, in fact you are funding it. You must care enough not to care.

2. Control your ability to care

Care when you should and not when you shouldn't. We care about the strangest things. We care more about dogs than we do people. When a person kills a dog, it's on the news and the person involved is over vilified and the media attempts to destroy his life and the lives of those dependent on him. We seem to care more about what money can buy then what it can't. Money can buy cars, jewels, clothes etc., but it can't buy trust, loyalty, morals, happiness, etc. Care when it makes sense to care not when it doesn't.

***

Prison Piranhas Helped Me Learn That…

Friends Will Change Before Enemies

When we have friends, we all will go through good times and eventually bad ones with them. Today we will be BFFs, and the next day we will be enemies. With enemies, we know where we stand – yesterday, today and tomorrow.

Friends change from friends to enemies from enemies to friends. There is so much emotion and expectation wrapped into a relationship when people call themselves friends. Emotions run wild, causing rifts in the relationship. Expectations go unmet, causing friends to turn into enemies. Following a fall out there is a talk where parties explain themselves, an understanding is reached and reconciliation ensues. Up and down, from friends to enemies and back again. After all the talking, explaining, understanding and reconciling is another round of emotions getting out of hand and expectations going unmet.

With enemies, on the other hand, we start out as such and maintain that role. We both know where the other stands. There isn't any misunderstanding or anything to talk about. No reconciliation, just the same old thing of doing what enemies do.

Life Lesson

As I sat in prison, I watched youngsters bond, become friends and form cliques. They seemed so inseparable. However, these crazies were like piranhas. In groups, they would attack anyone who showed a weakness. An exposed weakness was like an open wound leaking blood into the Amazon

River sending the ferocious razor toothed fish into a feeding frenzy. In similar fashion to piranhas, these youngsters would turn on their friends if they became wounded by showing a weakness.

I was in a cell house with this group of wild youngsters who had all come from a prison called The Farm. They had a guy in their clique who would do all of their tattoos. They were all thick as thieves until the tattoo man let the smallest dude in the dorm take the commissary he was paid for a tattoo then he ran from a fight with an older prisoner.

Later that day, when we came out for chow, the tattoo man's clique turned on him. The tattoo man checked in because of the threats from his clique and never returned to the cell house. His "friends" turned into his enemies. They ransacked his cell and took his belongings ranging from his TV to his toothbrush.

These youngsters taught me how costly it can be to

have friends. It's better to know where you stand and not have to worry about the inconsistency friends can display. With enemies, especially in the joint, there is a level of respect that results in understanding. You both understand that when given the opportunity you will try and do one another in.

Summary

Before an enemy becomes your friend, a friend will become your enemy.

Action

1. Define boundaries

People always will interact with others they consider to be their friends. However, boundaries can be established within the relationship and expectations understood. For example, when people become friendly, they can become contemptuous and begin to take liberties. I see groups of friends referring to each other as b!@%#es. I don't think

you should call anyone you have respect for a
b!@%#. Boundaries need to be set; if not, one day a
friend won't be in the mood to be called a b!@%#,
and now your friend is your foe. This goes for
taking liberties as well. Helping yourself to your
friend's resources, no matter how trivial, gets old
and annoying and results in a falling out.
Boundaries keeps in check the little things that build
up over time and prevents friends from turning into
foes.

2. Set internal boundaries

We must have our own boundaries or rules that
dictate how we interact with our friends. For
instance, we should have rules that determine what
we share with our friends. I don't care who you
think your friend is, you cannot tell him or her
every single secret, good or bad. People make
mistakes and bad judgment calls, and they can't
hold water. In addition, perceptions are different.
You can tell a friend something in confidence that is
a big deal to you, but to your friend it doesn't seem
to be that big of a deal, and she shares it with

someone. Once you find out, you are angry and upset with your friend and have a falling out. If you had those internal boundaries and rules, you may have had some prudence and not told her your business.

***

Because Prison is a Wilderness I Learned…

Appearance, Not Reality, Reigns

How a thing appears is more important than what
that thing really is. We have learned to spin things,
be politically correct, and to keep our "fronts up."
People are trained to make things appear other than
what they are. Appearance is king.

Take any politician and you have a person who is
going to the extreme to appear a certain way. How
he or she appears is more important than the truth
about that person. We as a whole are fine with the
appearance. We must be fine because we don't

attempt to find out the truth or the reality and consume the appearance.

Early on we learn to spin reality to make it appear prettier than what it is. We learn to utilize euphemisms as part of our spin game. When we are asked about a person or experience that we didn't find enjoyable we say they were or it was "interesting." We use political correctness along with other tools to appear a certain way.

We go through many motions to keep our fronts up and appear more important than we really are. I had a buddy who was good at keeping his fronts up. At face value, he looked as if he was doing well. He had the latest fashion accessories, a car, a dope sack, a knot in his pocket, and attached himself to real D-boyz. However, behind the curtain he was broke living from sack to sack and host to host.

Creating appearances and obscuring reality is a profession. You have PR firms in the business of helping their clients appear a certain way. Stagers or designers set up an area to make it appear larger, more pleasant and valuable than it is. Reality is covered up, hidden and replaced by appearance. It is less valuable than appearance; in fact, reality is nearly useless. Appearance reigns.

Life Lesson

I learned early into my prison sentence the value of appearance. Prison is like the wild. In the wild, you have animals that employ a tactic to look bigger or fiercer than they really are. Some even try to look weaker to attract prey then turn the tables.

In prison, the same goes on. I learned that appearing big, strong and indifferent reduced the likelihood of being tried. As soon as I touched down in prison, I began getting my weight up. I gained 20 pounds a year for the first three years of my incarceration, stayed working out and kept to my business. Not too many people could gauge how I would react to certain situations. Couple that unpredictability with my build, my indifference, and my solitude, and I didn't have too many problems. In the wild, an injury could mean death. As a result, animals try to avoid fighting by appearing strong in order to maintain their position and their life. Even if they win a fight, chances are they will render themselves vulnerable. Showing your weakness in prison is an injury that renders you vulnerable.

There was a guy in prison who appeared to be a devout member of the Muslim community; a community respected for its unity, search for knowledge, uprightness, and discipline. This guy became a Muslim after coming to prison. Anyway, he went back to court for another case. Unfortunately for him, it was a publicized case and his picture appeared in one of the cities' newspapers along with the details of his case. Instead of a devout, disciplined, upright member of the Muslim community he was exposed by the article in the paper. He had broken into someone's house, kidnapped a little toddler, took her to a wooded area, raped her, choked her until he thought she was dead, and then covered her body with leaves. The little girl wasn't dead and was found wandering some road abused, lost and scared. In Indiana, when you go to prison they take your DNA. Since this guy was already in prison on another case, they had his DNA and charged him with the crime, once they got around to testing it. Once this came out, he lost the backing of the Muslim community and the respect of the prison population. When he returned from court, copies of the newspaper article were in every dorm. His weakness was exposed, he was threatened, had all of his belonging taken and had to check in.

No one is quick to get his weaknesses exposed so we let our appearances reign not the reality.

Summary

Reality is replaced by appearance creating a new pseudo-reality.

Action

1 Appear

We all participate in the game of appearances one way or the other. We are either complicit in someone else's appearance game by not exposing them or we actively help someone appear to be what they really aren't. We might as well use that skill set to our advantage. We need to appear as if we are where we want to be, practice until we actually get there. They say behave like a king and people will treat you like one.

2. Create

Create your own reality. Currently we may not have the things we want in life or be where we want in this world. However, we have to have a vision that ignores our current reality. Once that vision is acted upon, it creates a new reality, your own reality. I have always wanted to be a business owner. However, I didn't have the knowhow or the resources to start a business. I did have the vision, so I ignored my current reality of being resource poor, ignorant and having no ownership and formed an LLC. I created a reality where I am a business owner. No one knows I have formed an LLC, so they are still living in a different old reality.

***

I Learned From Sexual Predators To…

Never Take Anything From Someone You Don't Want to be Bothered With

The first time you take something from a person, you are in debt. The door is open for them to come into your life. When I say take something, I mean two things: if someone hands you money or anything of value and you take it you're in debt; and if you allow someone to do you wrong, you are taking something from them that is intangible and you are in debt. If you don't want someone knocking on your door treating you as if you owe, don't take anything from them.

Nothing in life is free. Everything has a price and a string attached. There are no free lunches in this world.

When you are in the club and someone buys you a drink, you are in debt. That debt might be paid with conversation, a dance or sex. The same is true when someone takes you out and pays for dinner and a movie.

If you allow someone to mistreat you, then you are in debt to them. They believe that if you let them get away with something once, you ought to continue to allow it. I have a cousin who used to hang around the neighborhood buying and smoking dope. He also would go around beating people up and taking their dope and money. The ones who allowed him to get away with his brigand tactics were continuously subjected to them. My cousin felt that his previous victims owed it to him to allow him to rob and abuse them.

Life Lesson

When I got to prison, I didn't have anything. My celly had all the artifacts necessary for doing his time comfortably. He had a TV, radio, food etc. To use his artifacts, I had to be bothered with him. That is, I had to talk to him, play cards with him, and be in debt. I forced myself to tough it out until my money arrived to get my own artifacts. I didn't have to worry about being bothered with my cell mate because I wasn't in debt to him for using his things.

In prison, people like to engage in what I call "Feed'em and cut'em." They look out for you or give you things like food, radios, TVs, shoes or whatever you desire. Later, they will try and get something from you. If you deny them, they will talk bad about you. Some dudes will give certain people (ones with homosexual tendencies) nearly everything their heart desires hoping they won't pay it back. At the point of default they won't take anything as repayment except sex or violence. If the person doesn't acquiesce and give up their behind, then they will experience violence.

Some people will even buy debt. For example, if a guy likes to gamble and finds himself with a debt he can't pay and happens to be soft, sexual predators will try and buy the debt. They will pay whoever the guy owes getting him out of that debt so they can increase their chances of turning him out or having sex with him.

If you don't want to be bothered don't take things from people.

There was this GED class in prison with these two youngsters who would harass other students in class. They would crack jokes about their classmates, play the dozens and disrespect them. No one would say anything, allowing them to continue with their antics. Every day they got bolder and bolder and more disrespectful. They acted as if the other students owed it to them to let them disrespect them. One day, they started up with a new student. The new student got up and left the room. He went and scouted out the bathroom. He returned, pointed at the first youngster and then the second and said, "You and you in the bathroom." They both sat there, didn't move and shut up. They never bothered the new student again.

In prison, calling someone to the bathroom or mop closet is like challenging them to duel by slapping them with a dirty glove. If you don't accept the challenge, you basically die a coward's death. Going to either location decreases the likelihood of correctional officers intervening. The new student didn't take their nonsense and nipped it in the bud. He turned them into the ones in debt.

Summary

Taking from someone is like feeding a stray cat, sooner or later they will be purring at your door with their hand out.

Action

1. Don't take gifts

There is no such thing as a free lunch. If someone gives you anything pay for it right then and there. If you can't pay for what is given. Don't take it.

2. Don't lay down

If you allow someone to mistreat you in anyway one time, expect it to happen again and again. When people get away with something they have a tendency to continue that something to the point of it becoming habit. They don't stop until they are compelled to. Don't take anything from anyone. Nipping things in the bud may cause a minor problem in the beginning, but not doing so will cause you major problems in the end and ongoing problems in the middle.

***

A Friend Caught in a Compromising Position Taught Me That...

Hard Turns to Soft

Things start out hard and may keep that state for a long time. However, sooner or later that hard thing will turn soft. This is especially true for people. A person may start out hard. That is, they may be in the streets putting in work, carrying their weight, getting money and holding water. Then somewhere down the road they will get soft. They will turn from the streets, be unable to carry their load and they will be struck with an overwhelming desire to turn on the faucet. Just as too much pressure will burst a pipe time will turn a hard thing soft.

Time offers people the opportunity to see things differently, experience different thing allowing dynamics in and between people to change. These changes can either make a hard person harder or a hard person soft. You see it often with old people. Some go through life mean as all get out only to get old and turn into a despicable meaner old person. Others start out mean as hell and as they get older have some paradigm shift and become the nicest person you'll ever meet.

A street dude can have a child or have some experience that will change him and take him from hard to soft. Change and a situation sparking that change will occur sooner or later.

The friend you confide in will eventually betray you as his/her situation, or the relationship changes. For example, you might tell your current friend about someone or something that you don't want anyone to know about. Your friend might keep it close to the chest while you are friends. However, as soon as you two part ways that friend will tell all that you have confided in him/her.

Life Lesson

One of my buddies I was doing time with was a stomp-down street dude. He was doing around 90 years. No matter where he went or what he did, he had a hawk on him. He was always ready to take it there. He adhered to street and prison rules and principles. Somewhere along the line he got soft and gave in to a taboo prison subculture. I found out he had gotten soft when a sergeant caught him in a cell performing a sexual act on another man.

I watched as once hard dudes told about murders that were long forgotten. They could no longer carry their weight or water. The load was too heavy and softened them up.

I was in the joint with this white dude who was a "time doing" convict, hard to the bone and spent most of his life in prisons. When they started taking and testing our DNA he was charged with some murders in another state. He was already serving a 65-year sentence in Indiana. The news, the faces of the people he killed, or leaving the Indiana prison system turned him soft. He had to get all that he did off his chest by implicating others in the crimes.

Hard will turn to soft. You can't bet the house on the back of anyone. Sooner or later, their back will give in.

Summary

Hard today, soft tomorrow.

Action

1. Don't tell

We have a tendency to tell people our secrets. Some things need to be kept to ourselves. If we can't guard our own secrets we shouldn't expect others to guard them, and they won't.

2. Don't do anything that will haunt you

As time goes by, we become softer and softer. If we do anything that will weigh on us as time goes by, we will fold under that weight, it is human nature. It is best not to do anything that will eat at our conscience because we will give in, no secret is taken to the grave before being passed on to someone.

***

No Limit Taught Me...

Not to Get Too Adapted to a Bad Situation

Humans seem too have an extraordinary ability to adapt. If we aren't careful, our ability to adapt can become a bad habit. If we get too accustomed to bad situations and circumstances, we may lose our ability or willingness to recognize and take advantage of good situations.

Prior to going to prison, back when I was a teenager I told myself I would commit suicide before I went to prison. I doubted my adapting skills. I didn't think I would be able to survive living under modern day bondage. However, when the time came to go I had no choice but to ride, killing myself wasn't an option.

My first time going to prison, I went in with a long sentence ahead of me. Many people go to prison for a couple of years their first time. I went with 52 and ended up with a 39-year sentence. With that much time, I had to adapt, settle in, and get comfortable.

Although I didn't get too used to prison I adapted enough to have my ability and willingness to recognize and take advantage of good situations become retarded, not completely lost, just retarded.

Life Lesson

While I was in the joint, I met a guy we called No Limit. I assumed they called him No Limit because he would take things with the correctional officers to the extreme, and this had nothing to do with the fact that he looked like a young version of the junk yard dog. If he got upset, he would cuss, scream, bang and fight until staff came suited and booted with a cell extraction team to forcibly remove him from his cell and take him to the hole.

No Limit got so adapted to prison life, especially segregation, that it became his niche in life. No Limit would lose his ability to cope with general population, prank out, and do something to get sent to the hole. He would get out of the hole and after a while do it all over again. He did this for the eight years he was in prison. He had maxed out on his sentence and couldn't be held in prison any longer without catching a new case. The prison was happy to get rid of him but No Limit was reluctant to go.

About two months later, No Limit was back in the same maximum security prison he left. He got out, caught a new case, violated parole, went through the whole due process, and came back to prison in two months. When I saw him, I was like "what the heck?" Here I was dying to get a second chance, and he just squandered his. He told me his story and finished by saying, "I don't have any family or anything out there; I am cool here." I left it at that. People deal with things differently because they see things differently.

No Limit wasn't an exception; many of my cohorts became institutionalized. They became too adapted to prison. They lost that fear that keeps us safe; that fear that has us twice as shy after being once bitten. They lost their ability and willingness to see and jump on a good thing.

Situations and circumstances will pass. We should power up enough to endure those present situations and circumstances, but not so much so that we can't power down enough to see all that the new situation has to offer. No Limit got so used to prison that he couldn't and wouldn't take advantage of the infinite opportunities the free world had to offer.

Summary

If you let your eyes get too adjusted to darkness,

you'll be blinded by light.

Action

1. Power up

There will come a time when we will be in a bad way. When that time comes, we have to power up and handle it. We have to do whatever we have to do to successfully come through that situation. Once we are through it we have to…

2. Power down

Whatever you turned on to get through your bad situation, you have to turn it off at some point. After you have finished cooking, you turn of the stove. If you leave on the stove, you run the risk of burning your house down. That thing or that mechanism you enabled to get through your tribulation can burn you down. It can keep you from moving forward and taking advantage of some of the good things that come into your life. I am having trouble powering down and letting people completely into my life. I don't want anyone close enough to let me down.

***

My Family Taught Me That...

There is a Difference Between Family and Relatives

We are just related to relatives. We get it in with family, the long way. Blood has us related, how we interact with and feel about those we are related to make us family.

There are plenty of people in this world that I share blood with, however, I don't know them and don't care about them. I don't know my immediate relatives. I don't know my paternal grandparents or most of their offspring and siblings. I don't know anything past my maternal grandparents and one of my grandma's sisters. All those people I don't know and some that I do know are simply my relatives. We are related by blood. There is no familial bond, and I wouldn't break my back for them – and they wouldn't for me.

Family, on the other hand, I know, love and will go to the end of the earth for. We deal with each other the long way. We played together, they babysat me, fed me, fought for me, looked out for me, they are family. How we get it in with each other transcends blood.

Life Lesson

Prior to going to prison, I was hanging with my cousins, aunts and uncles on my father's side. I didn't grow up with them nor did I have that familial bond with them. However, I made an effort to hang with them, be around them, and attempt to establish that bond. I made the mistake of viewing them as family.

When I went to prison, I learned that they were simply some people I am related to. They didn't have the time of day for me when I went away. However, when someone who was their family went to prison they made sure they had a place for them to call, made sure they had visits, and made sure they were alright. They did what family does for each other. I am not family, I am just someone they are related to. They made it clear what a relative is.

My family – the people that fool with me the long way – taught me about family. They traveled across the country several times to visit me, they kept in touch, and made sure I was straight. They let me know that we are family not simply relatives.

Summary

Relatives may be there when you don't need them, family will definitely be there when you do!

Action

1. Determine who your relatives are

When you know who your relatives are, you can deal with them in that manner and expect to be dealt with in similar fashion. If you expect to be treated like family by someone you are simply related to, you will be disappointed and vice versa. If you know what it is from the jump, you won't be let down nor will you be disappointing someone.

2. Determine who your family is

Be clear who the ones that are actual family; the ones who love you no matter what and will part seas for you. These are the ones you have to do the same for. Life is too short and resources too scarce to be treating relatives like family and expecting to be treated like family when you are simply a relative.

***

Hearing of Brown's Death by Murder Taught Me...

Not to Be So Preoccupied with Meeting My Current Needs That I Fail to Take Steps to Meet My Future Needs

Often we get so caught up in what we are doing that we fail to think about and plan for the future. We aren't thinking about how we are going to successfully meet the complexities the future will throw at us. When we are living life, we are caught up in the rat race, in the present. As a result, we are preoccupied with figuring out daily puzzles: How we are going to get gas in our car, food on the table, clothes on our back, getting our kids to school in the morning, and making it to this appointment or that appointment. We aren't thinking about how we are going to survive when we are old, unable to work.

There is a future. We must give it consideration. If we fail to do so I believe that it will look similar to or worse than our present, making it imperative that we not get so caught up in today that we forget about tomorrow.

Life Lesson

Just imagine yourself sitting in prison being absorbed with and doing years and years of things that don't and won't matter in the real world. For example, making hooch (prison wine), beating up some guy, checking people, and all the other things that people in prison get involved in. These things don't really matter on the streets. No employer that I have spoken with cares that I whooped Lil Nook Nook or was the penitentiary wine maker.

Unfortunately, as prisoners we get involved in

frivolous things as a way to escape, to make the time pass, and to meet our current situation's demands. There is a bit of advice given in prison when you get a big bit, you are advised to get you a knife, a TV and a boy. Some people actually take that advice, and their life literally becomes centered on those three things. The knife is to combat or initiate attacks, the TV is to occupy yourself when you are on lockdown in your cell, and the boy is to replace the intimate relationship you left behind on the streets. Before he knows it, he has spent many years on nothing outside of adapting or even flourishing in his current situation that he is unable to meet the impending demands he will soon face in the real world.

Ninety percent or more of those incarcerated will be released sooner or later. Many of them have been focused on surviving prison, not how they are going to survive after prison. They haven't been taking steps to overcome the new set of road blocks stacked on top of old road blocks and take advantage of what life has to offer.

Many of peers left prison with nothing to look forward to but a life of crime. They did not believe they could survive without it. To them, the future was bleak. All it offered, as far as they were concerned, was a cycle: crime, prison, release, and then repeat. The only thing that was going to break that cycle was death. They were the ones who didn't take the time to acquire real world marketable skills. They didn't learn about computers, finances, life skills or about how the real world works and how to navigate it. They spent their time caught up in their present.

The first prison I found myself in, I came across a guy who's last name was Brown. He was a real character. He had to be in his forties when I got to prison. He had corn rows like the youngsters and was bronze colored with European features. He wore tight state-issued thermal shirts with the sleeves cut and the remainder rolled up like the Fonz. He stood well over six feet with a muscular build and walked similar to Tomcat. He was, to me, kind of hyper aggressive, overbearing, and a bit mentally slow. His time was spent attempting to impose his will on people. He sharpened his tools for doing so by working out and talking crazy; I guess that was a civilized form of chest thumping and grunting. This is how he dealt with the day-to-day complexities of maximum security prison.

What he didn't learn was how to make it in the real world. All that chest thumping doesn't work in the real world. If you attempt to impose your will on someone in the work place, it is considered work place violence, even if it is simply talking out of the side of your neck. In the real world, the game being played is chess, and we have to learn to play. We have to push our pieces, use our pawns, strategies, facades, keep our fronts up, use our minds and think. We have to play the game how it goes. Brown got out and got himself murdered. He got out on that chest stuck out, hyper aggressive nonsense, and someone killed him. He probably scared someone to death, and they weren't going to live in fear, so they killed him.

Brown didn't take the time while in prison to learn how to navigate through life. Nor did he learn things that would help him meet his future needs. His most important and basic future need upon release was to stay alive. His preoccupation with satisfying his current need via hyper aggression and high-handed ways kept him from taking steps to meet his future needs and he ended up dead.

While you are in prison with your knife, television and boy or on the streets with your cars, lattes, and Gucci you need to be acquiring skills that will help you successfully meet the new and unpredictable demands of the future.

Summary

Use your abilities today to be able to cope with tomorrow!

Action

1. Learn to play chess

Chess teaches you to conceptualize and analyze. You must think about all the possible outcomes of a single move, determine which move is the best and just an ongoing series of conceptualizing, analyzing, weighing and deciding. You must be able to think three moves ahead. You have to think about your next move, how your opponent will move in response to your move, and what move you will make in response to the move your opponent made in response to your initial move. Life needs to have some similar thought process that makes a player successful in chess. Don't just think in terms of one move. Think ahead about your future moves. You don't want to put yourself in a bind. Instead, put yourself in a position to capture kings.

2. Take advantage of opportunities

If you are presented with opportunities to learn, then learn. You never know how useful that experience will be in the future. I learned to touch type in prison. At the time, I had no real use for the skill. However, it came to be a very valuable skill for my future despite it not having much value for my present at the time.

***

Seeing the Change in Myself I Learned That…

You Can Get Into A Situation and Lose Yourself

We will, sooner or later, be given the opportunity to lose ourselves. We will find ourselves in a situation that will somehow change us and give us a paradigm shift that is either positive or negative. I see this change all the time in women who have been in love with an unfaithful man. The women are usually very faithful, loyal and uninterested in having any other sex partner who is not their man. After putting up with years of unfaithfulness and all the drama and nonsense that goes with the unfaithfulness she gets lost. She gets lost in hurt, hate, and a host of emotions that transform her. She then mimics the actions of the one she loved and becomes unfaithful, promiscuous, and unrecognizable. She allowed her relationship with this man to change her for the worse.

Our self-losing situation may be different along with the change. However, the transformation still occurs.

Life Lesson

When you start a prison sentence you most likely will do it with a group of guys. That is, many people you meet in the county jail will become friends or acquaintances and so will the dudes you meet in prison pit stops like RDC here in Indiana. In addition, people you meet when you first get to prison will be part of the group you do your sentence with. You won't literally do your time together physically because some people beat their cases and go home, some get small bids and some get big ones and are sent to different prisons and get released at different times. I went to a maximum security prison, and it was years down the road before I ran into dudes I was with in the county and RDC.

Running into someone a decade or so later after he has traversed the prison circuit affords you the opportunity to see how it changed him, to see how he let prison make him unrecognizable to those who knew him before. I knew so many dudes who were inherently nice, they were understanding, naive, fun and forgiving only to become damaged by the situation (prison). Now they are cynical, full of hate, and don't care about anything or anyone including themselves.

I have changed a great deal as a result of prison. Prior to going, when I was running around the streets, I was caught up in this hood thing, and I wanted all of my guys to be prosperous and for all of us to be together a collective representing our prosperity and our hood. I tried to look out for a few of them and make a way for them to eat, hoping that one day we would take off. Instead, I went to prison. When I left for prison, the casket was closed on me because I had such a big bid, I felt like everyone turned their backs on me and left me for dead.

Feeling abandoned coupled with life in prison, I changed. In prison, resources are scarce, and it is every man for himself. My hood taught me that you are on your own, and prison reinforced that teaching. So I went from a person who was shorting himself so my friends could eat to one that is selfish. I became focused on me. I let the prison situation make me indifferent about everyone except myself. In prison, we fight and struggle over scraps and insufficient resources. We fight to get admitted into programs that offer time cuts but have limited openings, we fight over toilet paper, showers and blankets. If you aren't selfish and constantly looking out for yourself, you will always get the short end of the stick because the next man is cutthroat and has his eye fixed on his self-interest. After living this way and having that paradigm shift onset by having the casket closed on me by my hood, I became selfish and now don't really care about too many people or things.

As I write this, I am on home detention and interacting with the public, friends and family. As I do so, I can't seem to care about anything but myself. As I look at these people, I can't seem to care because I felt as if everyone has been living their lives doing them not caring about me; it was all about them when they were doing them. Now it has to be all about me. I understand the survival instinct that had them focus on doing them. My same instinct and need for self-preservation has kicked in and is in overdrive, and I am like "Forget everybody!"

Fortunately, I know things shouldn't be that way, and I have recognized my own transformation along with the ability of a situation to transmute. I also realize that we are all going to go through life and changes as a result of what we encounter during that life. However, we can take steps to see to it that our change is positive overall and that negative amendment is limited.

Summary

Change the situation; don't let it change you. If that is not an option, let it renovate you positively!

Action

1. Gain knowledge of self

Take a look at yourself. Do this by looking at where you have been, what you value, what you think, and what you think about, how you feel, how you react, and anything else you can think of that shapes and defines you. Use these things to determine who you really are and who you really aren't.

2. Change the situation

If you have a clear understanding of who you are, being changed by a situation becomes more difficult. Don't get me wrong you will be changed by every situation in some form, however, your core stays the same unless you allow it to be altered. With knowledge of self you have the ability to change situations and make them conform to who you are. Prison is an environment that can turn you into a criminal, a creep, and a weirdo. You can also use the situation to strengthen who you are by making it conform to that mission. I didn't smoke, drink, fornicate, rob or otherwise change for the worse in prison. I wasn't raised to value those things. I was raised to value learning; my grandma taught me to read when I was four. I was taught about hard work and struggle; my momma worked, went to school, and raised two boys as a single parent. That's who I am, and that's what I did in prison. I changed the situation from one of violence and crime to one of education and hard work. You can change your situation, too.

***

Seeing My Road Ahead I Have Learned That...

It Takes More Time and Energy Doing Things You Have no Business Doing Than it Does Doing What You Are Supposed to...

When you invest your time and energy in doing the wrong things, do you ever ask what else your energy and time is going to be invested in? It's invested in keeping from getting caught, keeping people from finding out, getting out of the trouble you spent so much time and energy getting into. When you do what you are supposed to do, you don't have to worry about covering it up, hiding it or getting out of it. Your time and efforts can be spent on the next project and moving forward to greater and progressively greater accomplishments.

This reminds me of those businesses that take shortcuts when creating a product to bring to market. On the front end they may have saved tons of money and time taking short cuts. However, when that product doesn't live up to standard, fails and causes injuries or some sort of harm all that time and money saved on the back end is wiped out. Now the company has to pay to have the repercussions of the shortcut they took, spun in a positive direction, the product recalled and to take care of the lawsuits.

Life Lesson

Being involved in crime, I had the opportunity to see people consumed with it. They were either actively engaged in crime or fighting to get out of the trouble caused by their involvement. Because a person goes to prison doesn't mean that they stop getting into trouble. I witnessed many dudes who did nothing but things that they had no business doing. Some of them got a good run before they were caught, but they got caught. All that time and energy put into the activities that got them in trouble was wasted. It was wasted because they weren't doing the things that they were supposed to be doing. If they were handling their business, they were set back: In prison, to leave before your EPRD (earliest possible release date) or get your time cut for programs, you have to stay out of trouble. A person can go through an entire college course, be on the verge of completing the course and receiving a 1-2 year time cut, and have it all snatched away because they got in some trouble.

On top of erasing everything they worked for, whether it was on the up and up or on the criminal side, they have to waste more time attempting to get out of the trouble they put so much time and effort getting into.

As I sat in prison, I had to analyze my situation and

concluded that if I had done all that I was supposed to, I would be better off. Not only would my road have been less tumultuous, it would have been shorter. If I had worked a job, saved, invested, and went to school, after 18 years I would be in a great position. However, I spent three years in the streets meddling then went to prison, which wiped out all that I spent those years trying to build. Then I spent 15 years involved with prison and its agents. For close to two decades of getting into trouble, looking over my shoulder, trying to not get caught, and focusing on getting out of trouble I have nothing to show for my efforts except felonies and obstacles created by my felonies.

As I sat in a small cell, all I could think about sometimes is how I made my life that much harder and about all the obstacles I will have to face once I am admitted back in to society. I keep telling myself that it would have been easier to have listened to my momma than to listen to the streets. It takes less effort to go to work every day while going to school then it does to duck and hide from the police, be locked in cages, and endure physical and mental tortures – tortures like being stripped down to your underwear, cuffed with your hands behind your back seated on a concrete floor in a cold building for hours, or locked in an isolation cell while staff tampers with your food, destroys the property that you hold dear to your heart and use to get through the prison experience with your sanity. Not only is it easier, it pays off in the long run.

Summary

A simple investment: do what you are supposed to, not what you aren't!

Action

1. Clearly state where you want to be

We all have some point in this life where we want to be. Clearly define that point so you know where you are going.

2. Make a list

List all the things that you are supposed to be doing to get where you want to be. Once that list is done, start checking things off as you complete them. This gives you a visual of what needs to be done and what has been completed. Hopefully it will motivate you to keep progressing forward.

***

Convicts With No Family, No Job, and No Formal Education Taught Me That...

For a Man to Survive, He Needs Hustle

The world is in constant motion. Nothing sits by idly during this motion, at least nothing that is worth anything. Any person who is not busy at work, whether it is work for hire or work for self, will be left by the way side starving or just over broke. Constant motion includes but is not limited to: increases in daily expenses like gas, increases in monthly expenses like rent, and changes to laws that affect survival. For example, they make laws stating people need to have certain credentials to work a certain job or that people with a certain background can't work in a certain industry. While constant motion takes place you best be hustling to stay ahead, to survive, and to flourish.

Hustle separates the living from the dead. Dead are those who sit lifeless and only move to receive a hand out. The living do what it takes to make a way for themselves and those dependent on them. The living are those people you see working multiple jobs, while gritting and grinding on the side whether it is doing hair, selling incents or bootlegs. Hustle is vital to a man's survival.

Life Lesson

In prison, sources of income are limited. You can either work, go to school, depend on someone from the streets to send you money, or you can come up with some sort of hustle. If you work, there are various levels of monthly income depending on the job. You can make D, C, B or A pay. D pay amounts to $10 bucks a month and A pay is about 25 cents an hour. I worked several A paying jobs and made between $10-$62 bucks a month because my hours varied. There are exceptions if you work for PEN products. You can make more even up to a few hundred dollars a month, but those jobs are extremely limited. If you get lucky and get a job paying you a couple of hundred a month, you will be taxed for room and board and other gimmicks to get your money.

Most people only make $10-$40 dollars a month. That money has to go to soap, deodorant, toothpaste and all the things that relate to your hygiene. What's left has to be used to supplement your diet. Yes, you are fed three meals a day. However, those meals aren't enough to sustain a grown man. I remember going to the hole for thirty days. In the hole, the only food you had access to was what they dropped in the slot. I starved every day. I sat real still to conserve energy so I could make it to the next meal. The longest stretch was when they dropped off the dinner tray at 3 p.m. and the next tray came at around 3 a.m. I lost weight rapidly. I realized that the small amount of food they give is only enough to keep you alive. What they feed needs to be supplemented by buying commissary.

With the limited monthly income in prison, you have to have hustle in order to eat, maintain your hygiene, and do other things like write letters. I had a job, some hustles, and someone sending me money. If I didn't have a hustle, I would have starved. Some people didn't work or have family willing to send them money. They either lost weight or got a hustle. I wrote papers, braided hair, and did personal jobs as they related to my job, for example; when I worked in laundry I washed peoples' clothes for a monthly fee, and when I was a clerk I made copies and typed legal work. The extra income helped me to keep from starving and do other things vital to surviving and flourishing.

Believe it or not, prices were increasing in prison and rules were constantly being implemented that were affecting how we lived in prison. They limited who could send us money, what jobs we could work, the number of jobs we could work, the credentials we needed to work certain jobs, and all sorts of reactive rules and policies. As a result, the living had to stay in motion – that is, us convicts had to constantly be finding and revising hustles. As one hustle got knocked or more complicated, new ones had to be formulated or reworked. I am reminded of the time when we were being constantly dropped via urinalysis with those cups that instantly determined if you were dirty. This new cup and the frequency of drug testing put a dent in the weed man's hustle. So he switched it up and started selling K2, that synthetic lab weed. The main selling point was that it couldn't be detected via drug screening. Despite his hustle being reproachable, he kept it moving because if he didn't he wouldn't have survived.

Sitting in a cell and watching the financial situation of my peers in prison, I realized how important hustle was. Many of my peers didn't have anything– no family, job, or formal education – just their hustle. Instead of starving, they conjured up all sorts of hustles. How can a man survive without it? This world is so volatile and shifty that a man can have his job today and lose it tomorrow taking his home, car, and whatever else he maintains through the income his former job provided. That's why hustle is so important.

Summary

If you don't have a hustle get one, if you got one calibrate it accordingly, hustle is survival. When it is calibrated, it is prosperity.

Action

1. Determine what you know

We all know something as a result of trekking through life. I played in the streets selling drugs and doing many other things. I also have spent many years in prison. These two subcultures have taught me a great deal about right, wrong, life, perspective, good, evil etc. Now I have to find a way to…

2. Monetize that knowledge

Turn what you know into dough. You can write books sharing your experiences, do consulting, create a website, or if you have a trade you can do that for extra cash on the side or turn it into a full-blown business. Turn what you know into your hustle.

***

Red Taught Me To...

Watch What You Eat

When I say watch what you eat, I am not talking
about dieting or literally watching what you put in
your mouth and consume as nutrition. What I am
talking about is what you feed your mind. The
things you read, the things you listen to, and the
things you see, process, and ponder on or think
about are things that you feed your mind.

Some people sit around all day consuming some
sort of media. That media shapes their entire
perspective. When I use the word perspective, I am

talking about all that word encompasses: your viewpoint, outlook, perception, how you take things, how you assess things, etc. For example, some people watch news related media and depending on which news media outlet they watch their perspective becomes either right-winged, left-winged or some variation of those schools of thoughts. They will begin to talk like a left- or right-winger using terms and phrases popularized by these groups. They will begin acting like members of these schools of thoughts. They will begin consuming products associated with these schools of thoughts. You can also look at kids who consume reality show based media. Their perspective becomes shaped by, in tune with, and a replication of the particular reality shows they eat.

Because our nature is to allow information, experiences and other things to alter, define or in some sort of shape or fashion influence our perspective, we need to be extremely careful and particular about the things we eat, the things we feed our mind. I learned this while sitting in prison listening, reading, watching and being bombarded with all sorts of information from all sorts of origins.

Life Lesson

In prison, I learned to watch what I eat, literally and figuratively. People I did time with weren't careful about their consumption habits and ended up flying over the cuckoo's nest. I met so many guys at the beginning of their prison sentences and had the opportunity to see them many, many years in to that sentence after they have changed. Most of them have adhered to some ideology propagated and sustained by a sect, religion or gang. The ones who didn't go crazy because of adherence to some group's ideology did so with the help of drugs.

There was this young kid from Kokomo, Indiana, who came to a maximum security prison when he was about 17 or a fresh 18. He was a skinny white kid with red hair. He was sentenced to 100-plus years. He was a kid who was scared, impressionable and going through that identity moratorium thing. He was embraced by many of the black guys in prison, most of them protected him, and genuinely liked him. Others wanted to take him sexually. After a few months, Red, as we called him, was moved to the other side of the prison fence. The prison began housing juveniles who were sentenced as adults. They kept them in a cell house separated from the adults. The next time I saw Red, he was a tattooed patch wearing member of a prison gang. He ate the ideologies of this group and went from hanging with Blacks to hating them. I have listened to some of the recruiters for gangs speak, and they are very gifted, and the group he became part of has some of the best.

The problem is that as we get older, acquiring more knowledge and experience, we will have a paradigm shift and our outlook on individual issues and on life will change. These gangs in prison will discard you for any minor infraction and become your enemy leaving you with nowhere to turn. When I left that prison, Red was still on good terms with his gang, however, that will have to change. It will have to change because of a growth process. As Red grows, he will outgrow his place within that gang. That growth will most likely not be supported by those represented via that tattoo on his back.

This happens as well to people who get involved with religion. I had a buddy get so wrapped up in some form of Christianity that he became too holy to be around anyone. The information he consumed on the subject was digested incorrectly, and he basically went mad. There was another guy who became a member of a Black Muslim sect, and he became so fascinated with one of their conspiracy theories that dealt with the government, sovereignty and the social security program that he went loony too.

Those who steered from the teachings of the sects went for the drugs. I had one friend who would take the medicines passed out at the prison's med window. Keep in mind that a third of the population where I was housed was diagnosed with some sort of mental illness. At the med window, they passed out various medicines for these issues. Guys would feign taking them and then sell them in the dorm. The meds would be of varied colors and earned the nickname of skittles once normal-minded people began taking these drugs. My friend was damaged mentally by these meds and became a totally different person who will soon be diagnosed as having a mental illness and required to take some of the skittles he used to buy.

Summary

Just as our body needs nutrients, so our minds need to eat as well. Our bodies can be poisoned by what we eat, and so can our minds. Don't consume poison.

Action

1. Create a filter system

We come in contact with so much propaganda and lies wrapped in truth that if we are not careful we can come to believe the hype and the lies. A system is needed to filter out some information so we won't have the opportunity to consume it. It's kind of like sitting in your living room and the Maury Povich show comes on. If I don't turn the television off or change the channel before I hear the story of a woman who has been on the show six times with 18 different men, none of whom were the baby's father, I will sit there and waste an hour of my life watching and consuming. My filter system is proactivity: I change the channel before the lies wrapped in truth and the propaganda even starts. That means shutting someone down before they even get started telling me about gossip or some other nonsense.

2. Create a system of critical thinking

As with any other filtration system, some things

will get through the filters. At that point, you need some redundancy to filter out what has snuck through. For the mind, that can be a systematic way to think about things critically. For example, you can have steps to break down information that has gotten through your filter:

i. Facts - Determine the facts

ii. Interpret – Organize facts and ideas to discover the relationship among them

iii. Analyze – Break information down and understand how each part relates to the whole

iv. Synthesize – Combine ideas to come to a conclusion, form solutions and design an action plan

v. Evaluate – Determine the relative value, truth and/or reliability of things

vi. Apply – Use what we have learned in one situation and apply them to other situations.

Create a system that gets the garbage out because

one way or another some trash will get in.

***

I Learned From a Man With Super Human Strength That...

Life Doesn't Always Test Your Strengths; It Often Tests Your Weaknesses

When we are in a battle, struggle or trying times, our enemy, our road block, or the cause of our tribulation doesn't target our strengths. We are like a fortress, and when attacked our strong points are avoided and our vulnerable areas are targeted, exploited and used to the advantage of our attacker. Life is no different: it finds the areas where we are weak and goes to work.

Look at people with nice incomes, they have plenty

of money coming in, beautiful family, great career and opportunities in abundance. Where are they attacked? Where they are the weakest. Their health is attacked or their greed is attacked. They get sick or their debt gets out of hand or they bend a rule to make more money. Whatever our weaknesses, are they are very often tested by life, and our weaknesses are likely to fail the tests.

Life Lesson

Many of my prison peers were very strong physically. They got plenty of rest, worked out religiously, and the diet they were forced to eat made some contribution. I am reminded of a guy that was housed in the SHU (Secured Housing Unit) or solitary confinement, as it is known. When I first went to prison, I had a kitchen job working in the SHU, and you could hear the guards gearing up to tumble with this guy named Bethea. They would eventually get the best of him after a great deal of effort, more effort than the stipend they were paid for their 12-hour shifts was worth. Eventually they quit attacking the fortress: Bethea was a fine physical specimen, muscular, veiny without a visual ounce of body fat, which is baffling to me because you will definitely lose weight in the hole. I went for 30 days and visibly lost weight. To make matters worse for the guards, his limited mental capacity was compensated by his superhuman strength. He could break out of handcuffs and tear through a straitjacket that was marketed as indestructible.

The guards stopped attacking his strength, which was his physical power, and started in on his weakness. His weakness, like all of ours, was his belly. To get Bethea to comply, they would basically starve him. Once he was extremely hungry, they would use food to either calm him down or get him to do what they desired. They attacked his weakness. For the guards, battling with this opponent on a physical level was very hard and dangerous. On top of having to tussle with a super strong adversary they had to call a nurse, supervise that interaction, move him from on location to another, then do all sorts of paperwork before they went home. A 12-hour shift could easily turn into a 14-16 hour shift.

Bethea's mind had been attacked by life's circumstance. It wasn't as strong as his body was. As I have mentioned before, prison has the ability to break the minds of people. Bethea was one of those people. Life attacked his weakness despite the increase in his physical strength.

Many of my peers were strong physically. However, they were tried and tested at their weak point. Some of my peers were weak in the flesh. That is, they couldn't live without some form of sexual contact with another person. They were so weak in that area they would stick their members in a soggy mop, a slaughter house mop at that. They couldn't resist the sexual temptations placed before them. Life seemed to place pressure on their weakest point until they gave in. It didn't bother with their strong points. Life knows that once your fortress is penetrated via your weakness, that your strengths will eventually come tumbling down as well. For example, my sexually active prison peers eventually stopped working out, burned bridges behind their sexual appetite, and some even contracted diseases that attacked the body.

Don't make the mistake of thinking that fortifying your temple by strengthening your strong points will successfully beat back an attack. Life will go after your weakness.

Summary

Life doesn't test to see if you are strong it tests to see how weak you are.

Action

1. Know

Know your weaknesses. If you know your weaknesses you can take steps to strengthen them and protect them. Until you build up that weakness and defense you can...

2. Disguise

Fake it 'til you make it. Act as if you don't have any weaknesses or make them look like your strengths. One of my weaknesses is speaking. Sometimes what's in my head differs from what comes out of my mouth, causing me to stutter. So I joined Toastmasters. Not only did I build up what was a weakness, I hide it behind confidence, a willingness to step up to a podium, and the content of what I am talking about.

3. Contingency

If your weakness is compromised have a plan. For example, when I had a speech to give, I would memorize the points I wanted to make and this allowed me to deliver an extemporaneous speech that seemed natural as opposed to sounding as if it was being read word for word. If for some reason I began fumbling or forgot something and my weakness began to expose itself I would jump to something I know in and out, a personal relevant story. My contingency was to talk about something I was very knowledgeable about, that way I could speak with confidence and expertise, compensating for and covering up my weakness in speaking.

***

Hustle Man Taught Me That…

A Grown Person is Going to Do What He Wants

As adults, we have a sense of entitlement. That is, we feel that we have earned the right to do what we want simply because we have come of age. We don't have to listen to what we are being told. We don't have to listen to any suggestions we are offered. Then we get an attitude when someone does tell or suggest something to us. Why we catch an attitude is beyond me because despite all the telling and suggesting, we are still going to go out and do what has already been made up in our mind.

Picture a wife giving a husband a laundry list of things to do while she is away. When she returns, the only thing taken care of on that list is what the husband wanted to do, if anything at all. Why wasn't that laundry list taken care of? Because the husband spent his time doing what he wanted to do.

I don't care what carrot and stick method you come up with, what coercive tactics you use, or what forms of trickery you implement, when it is all said and done an adult, with her sense of entitlement, is going to do what she wants.

Life Lesson

I learned this lesson in prison watching my peers operate, reflecting on how I operate, and watching how people in the free world operate, especially in relation to someone confined.

Despite all the laws and all the penalties for breaking the laws that are in place, there are boatloads of people who continually break those very laws. I once met a guy named Hustle Man. He was around five-two, half-bald, and would sell any and everything. He would run around the cell house selling everything from a slice of bread to electronic products. He was one of those guys who didn't have anyone looking out for him, and he couldn't keep a job because he was too busy looking for things to steal and then sell. Hustle Man was one of those guys who did what he wanted to do despite laws and consequences. He was back in prison on a parole violation. That's no big deal, however; he did a couple of decades in prison as part of a life sentence he was given. He earned a second try and was released on parole. He then proceeded to do what he wanted to do and not what the courts and his parole officer wanted him to do. As a result, he ended up back in prison, indefinitely.

When I look at myself, I notice that I do what I want to do at times. For example, I was taking this college course, and there was this group exercise the class was instructed to participate in. At that moment, I had no desire to do the assignment. All I wanted to do was get some other things done and that is what I did. The teacher was perplexed because I was one of her best students refusing to do the work she assigned. When she asked me why, I told her that I felt like doing something else. It was that simple I just wanted to do what I wanted to do. Nothing she or anyone could have or would have said that would have made me do anything other than what I wanted.

Remember my girlfriend that had a baby by another man while I was in prison? The entire time I was sitting in the county jail, she was doing what she wanted. She didn't do many of the things I told her to do. Instead, she was buying cars with my money, propping up her soon-to-be-baby-daddy with my resources, and ultimately making a child with some other man. Half the prison system is dealing with people who are grown; be mindful that a grown person is going to do what they want to do not what you want them to. They are never home when you tell them to be so you can call, they don't pick up when you tell them to, they don't come see you when you tell them to, they don't run the errand when you tell them to, it seems as if they don't do anything except what they want. When they do pick up, when they do visit, when they are home and when they do bust that move for you, it is because they wanted to do it. I used to listen to dudes screaming and hollering on the phones with their girls and sometimes their mommas because their girl or momma won't do what they want them to. They didn't understand that people have their own lives to live and doing what they want adds some fulfillment to that life, so that is what people are impelled to do.

Hustle Man finally had the opportunity to do what he wanted to do, and he did just that. He spent so many years being denied the things he wanted to do that he jumped on the chance to do them no matter the consequences. He added some fulfillment to his life even though it was brief and ephemeral.

Summary

You can think whatever you want, and that is exactly what an adult is going to do – whatever he wants.

Action

1. Get some understanding

Take time to understand whatever you can. With a better understanding, you will interact with reality better on many levels. In this case, once you understand how adults think and work, you will interact with them better. A grown person is going to do what they want, it's that simple. If you can understand that then you can…

2. Make them want to do what you want

Not too many people like to get up and go to work at a job they hate every morning, but they do. Why do they do it? They do it because they want a paycheck. An employer makes an employee do what the employer wants. When dealing with adults, we can't force them to do things, as that's a crime. However, we can appeal to their interest and make them want to do what we want or need them to do. Outside of making it worth an adult's time, they are only going to do what they want, not what we want.

***

Having So Many of My Own, I Learned That...

No One Wants to Hear About Your Problems

Everybody in the world has one problem or another. The last thing they need or want to hear about is another problem. People love listening to solutions. People pay pretty pennies to learn of a solution to their problem. It doesn't matter if it is solving weight loss, debt, lack of income, poverty, or problems with oil stains in your drive way, people will pay. What they won't pay for is listening to problems. In fact people charge hundreds of dollars an hour to listen to your problems.

When you are recounting to your friends how bad things are going for you and about this issue and that issue, they really don't want to hear it. They have their own problems to deal with. What they hope to hear after you have ran down your problem is how you did or plan to solve it.

Life Lesson

I went to the joint while still a kid. I didn't really know myself or how to make it in the world as a normal person. On top of that, I had three decades to do in prison if things went bad and a decade-and-a-half if things went good – neither scenario was good. Needless to say, I did not want to hear about, nor did I care about what someone else was going through. I had a few problems of my own to worry about.

A funny thing happens in prison: People love to share all that is going wrong in their lives. We all become crybabies and therapists. We vent, and we listen. We get jaded then we get upset as a result of continuously being inundated with our own problems and the problems of others.

One day, I was sitting at a card table playing a game of chance with Footie. He was crying to me about one of the thousand problems he was having. Sitting in earshot was a guy we called Nitti. Nitti had been listening to Footie tell me of his problems. Out of nowhere, Nitti, who was not part of the conversation or the game of chance, said "Shut your b!@%# ass up, always crying!" In the joint, calling someone a b!@%# is like slapping a man in the face with a soiled glove in the seventeenth century. Well almost, it didn't lead to a duel with loaded muskets. To make a long story short, they ended up in the mop closet fighting, sort of. Poor Footie couldn't stand the onslaught of punches raining down on him. Nitti had perfected the art of close-range, catch-you-off-guard, closet combat. He would go in the closet first, wait for you to step in just enough for the button man (the guy watching the door) to shut the door behind you then unleash a barrage of blows. If he caught you anywhere squarely, you would be unable to recover. Footie got out of there before he was caught square. Others weren't so lucky and had to take a trip to medical and explain how they came to need stiches as a result of a basketball game.

What I learned was that Nitti got tired of hearing about problems…so tired that he wanted to fight in order to not have to hear them. Fortunately, the rest of the world isn't as rude and violent as Nitti. I suspect they are just as fed up, though. I found myself rolling my eyes in the back of my head while on the phone listening to someone tell me all that is wrong. I tried to not get in someone's ear and tell them about all that was wrong in my life. If I did the next time I called, they probably wouldn't accept the collect call.

What wasn't in the diatribes circulating around prison were viable solutions to the never-ending problems we seemed to have. Everyone has problems, but only a handful of people have solutions. Those successful at problem solving are usually wealthy. Those successful at problem creation and propagation are in prison or broke.

Summary

Everyone has problems, maybe a few dozen, and no one wants to hear them, not even your closest friend or favorite cousin. However, they will listen to solutions to both your problems…that is, if you got'em.

Action

1. Talk about it

Talk about solutions, not problems. When people get together and talk about solutions, it turns into a brainstorming session. Sessions like these result in solutions and ideas. Both these things add value to individuals, groups and organizations. Crying about a problem doesn't do that, however. Don't get me wrong, I understand the difficulty in breaking away from crying about problems because we learned the value of tears early on. As kids, we cried, and adults catered to our tears and our problem of hunger, wetness or not getting what we wanted was solved. As adults, those days are long gone. No one wants to hear you cry about problems; they will, however, listen to you talk about solutions.

2. Implement it

Talk only goes so far because it is cheap. After you have brainstormed, put your ideas and solutions to work. Talk and no action is worse than simply no action. You wasted valuable time talking about something you are never going to do. You must implement your ideas and solutions. Even if they don't work you are one step closer to having a valid idea and/or solution.

***

A Check-In Taught Me That...

Never Do Things You Have to Run From

There has been a time in most of our lives where we have gotten involved with a situation that resulted in us either hoping that no one finds out about it or absconding to avoid the consequences of our involvement. I remember praying that my momma didn't find out that I shot my little brother with a BB gun. Later in life, I remember running from the police because I had a car full of guns, drugs and money. My life would have been simpler and less stressful had I not done things that I had to run from.

We do things that aren't criminal that leave us feeling like we have to run. For example, a guy came over to my house to install an alarm system. I spoke with him for a while and found out that he was from a different state. He left his home town running from his ex-wife.

There are several problems with running. One problem is that we don't have enough stamina to run forever. Another problem is that we can't run fast enough. Finally, even though we run the problem still exists. Running isn't problem resolution; it is problem avoidance. What this means is that, whatever you are running from catches up with you in some shape form or fashion.

Life Lesson

In prison and this life, there are people who are too slick for their own good. They seem to live to get one over on people. They run their little scam, get what they came for, and run before their victim becomes the wiser. There are also people who simply have poor judgment and get into things that are over their heads.

When I began my journey of incarceration, I was in the Marion County Jail. This jail has several cell blocks. Some are very old steel bar throwbacks from Lord knows when. Some of the cell blocks are newer, most likely based on some relatively newer school of thought as it related to the housing of criminals. Some blocks were designated as murder/robbery blocks that housed people waiting to be tried or sentenced for either or both of these particular crimes. Other blocks were designated as medical blocks, segregation (dead lock), sex offender blocks, juvenile blocks, and blocks for whoever else needed to be designated. Nevertheless, they would still throw you in wherever there was a bed, unless prohibited by law. I was in a murder-robbery block with all sorts of crazies. Many of them did what came to be called block hoping. They would find a way to leave one cell block and go to another cell block. They would say anything from

being sick to being scared for their lives. They
would get sent downstairs to a holding block then
be reassigned and sent back upstairs to a new cell
block. Some people did this out of boredom, to get
to a block with their friend, or to escape danger.
Sometimes they got "put on the door." Usually
getting "put on the door" consists of getting beat up
by several people and compelled to pound on the
thin steel door while screaming for staff so they can
get you out of the block. You can hear the pounding
from nearly anywhere on the floor if you are on the
old side of the jail. The walls, where they are not
bars, are made of a thin steel material that flexes
and makes the sound reverberate and amplifies the
sound of the banging.

I knew this youngster that would run up his debt in
a cell block by either gambling or going to the store
man. A store man has a surplus of commissary,
food and hygiene items sold by the jail. He will loan
you an item like a bag of chips for two bags of chips
back. Or he will loan you two bags of chips for

three back. He will even loan you $25's worth of commissary for a $40 send-in. A send-in is where the borrower has his family put the money on the store man's books or jail account that can only be accessed to purchase things from the jail commissary. Once the youngster ate good, lost good, and reached a point he could not handle financially, he hopped to another block. He did this at least a half-dozen times. Eventually those he owed caught up with him. They had him beat badly by dudes from their hood. The block hopper had hopped to the wrong block.

In prison, people get in over their head and are forced to flee. You can't block hop in prison because if someone wants to get you, they can. You have to go eat, so they can catch you at the chow hall. You have to go to work, so they can catch you where you work. You have to go to the offender services building for school, medical or some other reason, and they can catch you there. You have to go to the recreation yard sooner or later, and they will get you there. You will have to go to the commissary line eventually, and they will get you there. The one way that seems to get you out of harm's way is to check in or go to protective custody. They will either put you in administrative segregation or send you to another prison away from the people trying to get you.

I knew a guy who had been in prison for many years and knew the drill. However, he went the wrong way and broke the rules. He was working in the recreation building and witnessed a stabbing sanctioned by a white prison gang. His co-worker was a convicted child molester, so the gang stabbed him up. The guy who witnessed it and several other potential witnesses were corralled to the SHU. This guy, a seasoned prisoner, told what he knew and claimed to feel some loyalty to his coworker. Now this prison gang was on his head. After attempting to get at him, he was moved to the other side of the prison. That didn't do any good because they had a presence there too. By the time I left that particular prison this guy was still a marked man wondering when the prison gang is going to strike.

Both of these individuals did something that they tried to run from. They taught me that there is no point in running because we can't run fast, long or far enough to escape wrong. The real lesson they taught me is that there is no point in doing anything you have to run from. Personally, I feel that I am a grown man who shouldn't have to run from anything or anyone. Not to mention, I am an old man who can't run and will get caught anyway. Like I told you before, if you can't handle the consequences don't get involved.

Summary

You don't have the ability to run fast enough, long enough, or far enough, so don't put yourself in a position to run.

Action

1. Don't Bite

Don't bite off more than you can chew, as the old saying goes. Some people have a tendency to get in over their heads. They take on too much and before they know it they are drowning and have failed. Most of us don't take one massive mouth-filling bite but instead a series of small nibbles and our mouths end up full and we choke. I recently got out of prison and seamlessly began accumulating bills: rent, phone, Internet, gas, lights, gym etc. They all just crept up on me, and now I am chewing with my mouth full trying not to choke. Don't bite or nibble unless you can handle it.

2. Chew and swallow

If you do happen to bite or even nibble, you have to do so either knowing you can handle what you bit off or doing all you can to chew and swallow what you have bitten off. Everything is an equation that can be solved. A full mouth is an equation that has an answer. Find that answer. I find ways to pay my bills, I can't run from them. I simply work and at the end of the day I won't have to run from that because it is an honest living. I can chew and swallow that.

***

A Recreation Room Stabbing Taught Me…

Don't be a Witness to a Murder

If you are a witness to a murder, chances are you were in the wrong place to begin with. When I say, "Don't be a witness to a murder," I am talking about wrongdoing of any kind. The likeliness of you being a witness is greatly decreased when you are doing what you are supposed to be doing. For example, if you are getting up going to work, to school, some extracurricular activity like sports or a personal development program every day you won't have time to be in places where a murder is likely to take place. If, on the other hand, you are hanging on the block or visiting a common nuisance, you are sure to be a witness shortly.

Do you know what happens to witnesses? They are involved in the crime. They are expected to tell what they know or be implicated as a participator or be charged with some sort of obstruction. Sometimes they are detained, arrested and erroneously charged with a crime. When they do carry out their duties, as a law-abiding citizen, they are discarded by the system they helped, labeled a snitch and run the risk of being met with some sort of revenge.

Life Lesson

In prison, there is always something going on. Someone is always either getting stabbed, hit with a lock, robbed, sexually assaulted, beat up, lied to, played, hurt, told on, or lied on. Something is always getting stolen, broken, smuggled in, and smuggled out. No matter what happens, someone saw something or knows something. In prison, one of your neighbors is always home and if his back is turned the cameras will pick up what he missed.

The story I just told you about the prison gang stabbing the convicted child molester in the recreation building is an example of why you shouldn't be a witness to a murder. The administration will do any and everything to get to the bottom of what they think happened. The first thing they will do is launch an investigation. That will consist of sending any and everyone who might have been directly or indirectly involved, anyone who might have seen it and anyone who should have seen it to the SHU. Whoever they send to the SHU could be there for weeks or months while the investigation lingers. That means: no visits; no commissary; no television; limited contact with the outside world; no work; no school; all of your belongings are packed up, damaged and or stolen; your cell and bunk (your home) that you customized for your comfort is filled with another prisoner and you are subjected to the horrible living condition of the SHU. You will go through this for simply possibly having seen what went down.

All the rec workers and anyone who could be identified as being in the building when the stabbing occurred were sent to the hole for several weeks. No one got out until they got some answers. No matter where those answers came from the first people to get out of the hole were suspected and credited with giving up information. The people who were charged with the stabbing stayed in the SHU. Those released who may have actually had something to tell whether they did it or not were labeled and even had a hit put out on them by the prison gang whose members were charged with the stabbing.

For being a witness to a murder, not only did they get sent to the hole and have their lives disrupted they were tagged as snitches and put in danger.

I watched this go down time and time again in prison. I learned quickly not to be a witness. When anything was going down that didn't involve me or mine, I got out of there so there wouldn't be any reason to round me up, take me to the hole and make me part of some year-long investigation.

I pretty much stayed in my lane and minded my own business. Once you get to meddling in the goings on of others, you end up witnessing too much. As a witness, you become part of the murder investigation and things can go downhill fast from there. If the murderer knows you saw, he will try to take you out or assume you told if he gets implicated.

Summary

Some knowledge is power, other knowledge could be disaster. Be careful what you come to know about.

Action

1. Do what you are supposed to do

Chances are if you are doing what you are supposed

to do, you won't be a witness to things you shouldn't.

***

A Staff Member Named Mr. Rosales
Taught Me That…

There Ain't No Love

In this world there exists two places. There is a place where love is, and there is a place where love isn't. In either of these places there exists appearances. You can be in a place of love that appears to be a place void of it. I bet at some point as a child or a spouse you felt like you were living in a home that had no love for you. Likewise, I will assume you have been involved in a relationship that you thought was full of love but was actually filled with hate in disguise. Imagine, a person who spent decades in a marriage then is devastated to learn his or her spouse had been cheating and had long stopped loving them. To make matters worse, that spouse continues to do things to hurt their ex.

When I use the word love in this case I am not talking about that agape love, unconditional love your momma has for you or that love shared by a husband and wife. What I really mean by the word love is: consideration and respect for or a sense of obligation toward a person you have interacted with or continue to interact with. These can be brief one-time interactions or the long term continual variety.

If I deal with someone or have dealt with them in the past, I will always attempt to show them respect. Whether we are on good terms or bad, I will give them careful thought when needed and do by them what is required based on the informal terms of our past or present relationship. If they looked out for me in the past, I will look out for them when I can and when they need to be looked out for, I will try and keep them in mind when I know of an opportunity, and I will not attempt to do anything that will hurt them.

When it is all boiled down a person is shown love
by being treated right; that doesn't include simply
appearing to treat someone right.

There exists two places in this world, one where
you are treated right or one where you are treated
wrong.

Life Lesson

I learned that there are people, despite their
designation, who will go out of their way to mistreat
you. Mr. Rosales, come to find out, was one of
those people.

Toward the end of my sentence I found myself in a
reentry facility. It was a prison designed to help
prisoners transition successfully back into society.
After awhile I got a job dealing with databases and
data entry. By the time I got this job Mr. Rosales
had gotten a promotion. He went from a counselor
to the facility's community liaison and volunteer

coordinator. He became the face of the prison and he dealt with all of the volunteers that came inside the prison. This was an important job because this particular facility had hundreds of volunteers, from churches, universities, businesses, outreach programs, etc. He would take residents from the prison out into the community to clean parks neighborhoods and even build houses for Habitat for Humanity. He acted as if he was on board with the reentry concept and the mission of this particular prison.

My job was to keep his database updated. He needed to know when new people arrived to the facility and other important information about them. His clerks would use this information to determine what services they needed and to create lists. For example, every month volunteers would come in and throw a birthday party for all the prisoners who had a birthday that month. Using the database a list would be generated with everyone who had a birthday in that particular month. In addition to updating his database, I was one of the guys he could count on to participate in food sales, coordinate the monthly birthday parties, provide tours of the facility to students from local universities and even participate in forums with students from these universities.

I was attempting to be a co-facilitator for one of the classes the prison had in conjunction with a local university, However, I left the facility and went to a work release center. Coming back into the facility was all but impossible. The professor I was hoping to participate in the class with worked diligently however, and I was allowed back into the facility.

Everyone was excited to see me back in the prison on different terms. Everyone except Mr. Rosales. I would have expected him to be one with the most excitement. After all, it is his mission to see us convicts have a successful reentry. Instead of excitement, his jaw dropped with disbelief and immediately slammed shut with barely concealed anger. Despite his feelings regarding my return the class and the ceremony went off without a hitch. Things went so well I was welcomed to come back for another class. That's where things went bad.

When I was allowed into the facility the first time permission was granted without Mr. Rosales's involvement. The second time consent was given despite Mr. Rosales's objection. I can only assume this rubbed him the wrong way. All I know is that I returned to the work release facility on a rainy Thursday night after work, and they said I was on restriction. That is, I could not leave the facility for any reason, including work. What I found out, after a week of confinement, was that Mr. Rosales had come to the facility under the guise that he was on official business from the prison as part of an investigation involving me and the professor I was supposed to facilitate the class with. He told one of the counselors something along the lines that I wasn't where I was supposed to be when I was scheduled to go to the prison. I suspect he said other things as well.

As a result of his actions my job was put in jeopardy. I could have been sent back to prison as a prisoner and I wasn't allowed to return to the prison to co-facilitate the class. Mr. Rosales lied, for whatever reason. Despite the nature of our relationship, one where he could always count on me, he tried to ruin my life. After the investigation into the allegations I was taken off restriction. Logs from the prison and emails between the professor and the head of the work release facility proved that I was where I was supposed to be when I was scheduled out. In addition, the truth came out Mr. Rosales was off the reservation acting without the knowledge of his bosses and was using one facility against the other to get his desired results. When asked by his superiors what he was doing at the work release facility to begin with he said he went there to drop off some mail for a resident that was transferred there. While there he just happened to run into a counselor and just happened to engage in a conversation about me.

Mr. Rosales taught me that the appearance of love is not the existence of love. A person must be full of hate to be capable of going out of his way to spread lies and misrepresent the truth using his position.

Summary

Hate can dwell where you think love should be.

Action

1. Get love where they love you

Fill up on whatever you need at home or wherever you are treated right or treated with that love or spousal love; doing so has two main purposes. First, you won't end up searching for or expecting something you won't find. Looking to the dog- eat-dog world for love or justice may leave you disappointed. Fortunately, I never looked to prison staff for justice or love, so I never made the mistake of thinking Mr. Rosales was my friend. However, I did make the mistake of underestimating what he was capable of doing.

Second, when you fill up on what you need where they love you, you won't soon run out of gas. I was fortunate enough to have family in my corner the entire time I was in prison. As a result I was able to use that love to compensate for all of the hate I was submerged in. After Mr. Rosales unleashed his hate on me and my good friend the professor I had to dip into my reserve of love. Having that reserve kept me from doing something really stupid.

2. Give love where they hate you

As opposed to searching for love or fairness in a den of hate be that personification of love, justice, fairness and treat people right. Do not fight hate with hate. I see people continually fighting fire with fire creating two losers. Do what is right to combat hate.

What Mr. Rosales tried to do to me is a reflection of where he stands in this world despite his designation and public persona. I can't fight his hate with the hate that he attempted to stir up in me. Instead, I chose to do what was right and that was to move on.

Doing what is right needs to be done at all times. You won't always know where they hate you. Because of that ignorance you have to always be showing love or doing the right things. I didn't know Mr. Rosales was harboring that hate for me. Luckily, I always did the right things during our interaction. If I had done one thing wrong, he would have sent me up the river the first chance he got. The chance he took didn't end quite like he wanted because I did what I was supposed to before I needed to.

***

A Guy Who Laughed at His 110-Year Prison Sentence Taught Me that There is a…

Conclusion

You can learn a lot from a dummy. I am a dummy who has learned quite a bit. Many of my lessons have been learned the hard way. One major lesson I learned is that life is too short to be learning all of its lessons the hard way.

The final lesson I want to share with you is that, there is a conclusion. All things come to an end; it is up to us to play a role in that end being positive or negative.

A guy I knew got out from under a 110-year prison

sentence for murder, and the people involved in my shooting attempted to pay him to kill me. He was in the paper for laughing at the sentence when it was handed down. He was notorious for robberies as well as murders. After getting his conviction overturned and going free, he was murdered in his hood. He made the mistake of thinking he was above conclusion. He didn't heed the lessons about life he had learned and helped others to learn. All the dirt he did wasn't reconciled until he was dead, and that dirt killed him.

Endings do exist. Don't make a mistake and think that all things go on for perpetuity. My man with the 110 didn't think his light would go out and thought his reign of terror wouldn't conclude. He found out the hard way that there is a conclusion.

Action

1. Plan

When one thing ends, that means another thing will begin. Plan for the conclusion and prepare for the beginning. I planned for the ending of my sentence by getting out of what we call "bid mode." It's a certain mind state, set of ideologies and ways of doing things that help you get through your sentence. Aspects of that mind state, those ideologies and ways of doing things aren't conducive to a successful life in the free world. I prepared for the beginning by learning how society was operating and finding out what skill sets I would need and actions to implement to make a successful transition.

2. Implement

Implement the aspects of your plan that will increase the likelihood of you not fading away with the conclusion of whatever you are involved in. If one part of your career or lifestyle ends be ready to move on to the next chapter of your career or life. I can't be free from prison physically and be stuck their mentally; I have to move on to the next phase just as you do or will.

###

About the author:

Edward Ball is the founder of Ball Team Enterprise LLC. He founded this company to help people extract lessons from their mistakes and the mistakes of others and use those lessons as personal and professional development tools. Through his eBooks and other informational material he aims to help people be the best they can be. He spent the last 15 years in prison and is an expert on making mistakes. After being sentenced to nearly 40 years in prison Mr. Ball earned two Bachelor's degrees, one in Liberal Arts-Human Interaction from Indiana State University and one in Organizational Management from Grace College. He extends the following offer to anyone with the ability and willingness to learn: Be better, do better...come learn with us, Ball Team Enterprise.

Connect with Edward:

• **Twitter: ballteamllc at http://twitter.com/ballteamllc**

• ballteamenterprise.com

• **www.facebook.com/ballteamenterprise**

***

Enjoy a preview of my second book:

What I Learned in the Streets and in Prison

That Can Help You Win at the Game of Life

Introduction

Game can be defined in several ways. However, there are two definitions of game I find important. The first definition of game is: Game is an occupation or business along with its rules and loopholes. The second definition of game is: Game is a calculated strategy or systematic plan. The fact is we all need to have some type of game to survive. We all need to have game because we are thrust into the ultimate game: the game of life.

Game is a business or occupation and is basically something we play. Some games have higher stakes than others. Not all games are legitimate. Selling drugs is a game, selling apparel is a game, creating software is a game and chasing men or women is a game.

People in these games and others, either have game or not. In other words they know how to play the game or they don't. If you don't know the rules and loopholes of the particular game you are in you can't successfully play the game. In fact, you really can't play the game at all; all you would be doing is messing up the game.

An accountant has game if he: knows all of the generally accepted accounting principles, the rules of his profession; the laws and the loopholes, helps you make money and decreases your tax burden. He has game because he is in an occupation/business within which he can do his job well. On the other hand if you deal with an accountant who doesn't know the ins and outs, GAAP's, tax law and the loopholes your tax burden may increase and you may even get audited. That accountant has no game, at least in the realm of accounting.

Another form or aspect of game is a calculated strategy or systematic plan. Whenever you approach an endeavor it is imperative to have a strategic plan. Only a person who is without game gets into something all willy-nilly. Something as simple as speaking to a woman requires a plan. The plan may be flexible and tailored to the woman. The plan may include what you are going to say and how you are going to say it. The ability to formulate an effective plan comes from knowing the rules of the game; and there are rules for speaking to men, women and even children. There are rules governing how you speak to certain categories of men, women and children.

CEOs of big and small businesses alike, operate them according to the strategic plan they created. A CEO with game gets in the game of business and makes it profitable. This CEO knows how the game goes or knows the rules, written, unwritten and the loopholes which allow him to create a great strategic plan.

Even crooks use game to separate you from your valuables. First of all, they enter into a particular game of some sort or specific type of crime; then they formulate a scheme to rob you and get away with it. They run game so good you are left in disbelief after you realize you've been had.

In actuality there are so many games to play within this game of life, and even more ways to play them, that you need to constantly be improving your game. This will allow you to be successful at the overall game of life. People with game know the rules of the game(s) and use those rules to their advantage. Since you can't know everything, a person with game should know his shortcomings and find teammates to fill the gaps.

You can be given game. Your parents give you game, so much game you should be winning at the game of life. But you probably didn't listen to the majority of the game you were given. Because you can be given the game, places like school have been created along with programs like apprenticeships and mentoring. In addition, you can get game from books.

In the first part of this book I give tid bits of game I think can play a role in helping you be more successful and perhaps a bit more cynical and suspicious in life. The tid bits in the second half of this book can help you avoid having some, not all, game ran on you. I think many of the bits of game in this book are familiar and most likely have been experienced by you. However, they may have been experienced differently or characterized differently. In any event they will be helpful to you.

If you know the rules of the game, have the ability and willingness to play the game how it goes and have the capacity to think critically and strategically you pretty much have game. You can recognize game when you see it and get in the game and play it successfully.

Game is a tool not a ruler. Rulers use game as a tool

I believe many of you are playing the game butt-naked: You don't have a uniform, a bat, shoes, a glove or teammates and that's why you are losing. As you start peeping game you begin to acquire gloves, bats and uniforms and you start building a team. Equipped with these tools you can play the game the way it was meant and increase your chances at success and avoid being struck out inning after inning. Hopefully this book will allow you to either start peeping game or add another dynamic to your game. You are either at the game or in the game. I want to help you change the game. If you are at the game you are being played, if you are in the game you are doing the playing. By changing the game you make others play by your rules.

I must give my readers a warning. I have spent over 13 straight years in prison. As a result my points of view, beliefs and perspectives may be skewed and way off the mark. However, everything I say is my reality created from my unique experiences.

***

SECTION I: The Game

Chapter1
Charge it to the game

Often you can get so caught up in an endeavor, person or thing that you can't let it go. You probably have invested so much that you feel it would be a waste not to continue. However, it may be better to cut your losses and move on. This is true for various reasons. First, when you let it go you are taking control. Second, you position yourself to take advantage of other opportunities. Finally, when you "charge it to the game" your focus shifts from what you want it to be, to what it is.

When I am playing a game my goal is to take control of my opponent. One of my tactics is to get out ahead of my adversary. Once I am ahead of him he is chasing me, all that he has lost and everything he has invested. Then I begin doing things to frustrate him. When he becomes frustrated he is no longer thinking clearly. Instead of walking away and charging his losses to the game he chases after them. He is out of control; he can't let it go and before he knows it he has lost everything including the game, his temper and his confidence.

The moment my adversary stops playing and charges his little losses to the game he nullifies my control. Also, he gains control over whether we will continue to play and control over his temper. Now he can get his mind right and play more of a role in determining the outcome of the game or move on to bigger and better things.

What is seen in many relationships are people who refuse to charge it to the game. They stay with their loser girlfriend, wife, boyfriend or husband even after nearly losing everything because of them. They refuse to cut their losses and move on. The result is that they miss out on that good man or woman and stay stuck with a sinking ship. Pimps use this tactic to keep their whores. They make new whores pay to get pimped. The logic is that if the girl gets the idea to leave the pimp she immediately begins to think about all the money and other things she has invested in, and for, this pimp. Seems like it would make more sense to stay with her investment than it would to move on and leave it all behind. Her attachment to things, her investment and her unwillingness to charge it to the game keeps her from gaining her freedom.

In life you can get involved in things that drag you down but because you have put so much time, money, sweat and tears into it, you can't or won't let them go and you miss opportunities. The wise thing to do would be to charge your investment to the game and take advantage of all the opportunities that come your way; opportunities you might otherwise miss while holding on to a sinking ship. At the very least, when you let it go or charge it to the game you are in the right state of mind and position to jump on other opportunities that come your way.

Prior to going to prison I was shot by someone I knew from the neighborhood. I was so caught up in making his life miserable and getting revenge that I couldn't let it go. I wasted some of the best years of my life in prison because I didn't charge it to the game. In addition, I repudiated a support system that would have helped me do anything in the world. However, I was so caught up in what I wanted it to be that I didn't take advantage of what it was.

I should have taken the shooting as a hazard that comes with being in the streets, left it there and moved on. Fighters know that when they enter the ring they can get knocked out. If they do get knocked out they don't go chasing down the guy that knocked them out trying to kill him. Good fighters simply charge it to the game of fighting; they move on, continue to train and keep fighting. When and if they face a fighter again they are better prepared to do the knocking out.

How to win: have game

You win by:
1. Taking control

2. Positioning yourself

Life is too short to be chasing what is already lost. You need to take control and let that lost thing go. If you have a hundred dollars and lose ten, you can't spend all day and the remaining 90 dollars trying to find the lost 10. You can miss out on the chance to make a thousand dollars because you are chasing that lost ten. Charge that 10 to the game and position yourself to grasp the opportunities around you.

Your focus needs to go from what you want it to be to what it is. Continuing with our example, what you want it to be is that you find that ten dollars. However you have 90 dollars and that's what it is. You should focus on the 90 before you lose that too. Some things need to be charged to the game.

***

Chapter 2
Roll or get rolled over

In the processes of handling your business there are a few things that need to take place in order to increase the likelihood of your success. First, you should part from anyone who hinders you from handling your business. Second, get away from people who do not want to better themselves. Finally, split from those who don't support your plans. If you do not roll away from these people, they will roll over you. If they don't roll with you then roll over them.

The first group of people that you should part ways with include: haters and thugs. A hater's purpose is to keep you from being successful. Haters hate, perhaps, because they can't do whatever it is that you are doing. Thugs are into so much nonsense that if you are involved with them you may get caught up in their nonsense. You run the risk of being robbed, incarcerated and/or murdered.

The next group of people you should get away from is the miserable unfortunates. A miserable unfortunate is a person who, more times than not, is in a bad mood and has a horrible attitude. This person is always involved in some unfortunate event and is constantly crying about how it is someone else's fault. These people are like magnets that attract all the unfortunate circumstances they can. All of these unfortunate events and circumstances become a schema in their mind that shapes their point of view, how they think about things and how they react to things. They become a catalyst for a negative unfortunate cycle of misery; if you are not careful that cycle of misery and misfortune will rub off on you. Before you know it you are a miserable unfortunate who has lost the focus and desire to actively try and, ultimately, reach your goals. The danger with this group is: they subtly and unintentionally ruin those around them. Leave these people in their own misery, especially if you are trying to make achievements.

We all know people who are content in their current situation. They are content even if that situation is dismal. Contentment is displayed through their unwillingness to actively get up and at least attempt to better their circumstances. Never mind the people always crying about how they want to, or will, do better and how they hate their situation. If they aren't taking steps to better themselves, they are content where they are, regardless of their crying about it.

Anyone who isn't trying to better themselves isn't trying to aid you in bettering yourself. These individuals eventually turn into haters. On top of becoming a burden and making it twice as hard for you to handle your business they will sabotage your efforts. This is the bottom line: if a person isn't trying to do anything for himself, he can't and won't try and do anything for you except take and take from you and if that fails, he will hate and hate on you. Your best course of action is to roll on.

There was this guy in prison they called Graveyard. He had an extensive prison sentence and will likely die there. He is a sexual predator homosexual who has murdered in prison and has stabbed or attempted to murder countless others. He isn't trying to do anything to better himself or those around him. All he wants to do is have sex with men and smoke weed. He doesn't have any qualms about sabotaging the efforts of those around him who are trying to make it home. He has nothing to lose and doesn't care if you lose what you have. He is the epitome of someone who will roll over you if you don't roll away from him.

There are plenty of people in your lives who don't support your plans. You need to burn rubber on them. People who don't support your plans basically cast bad vibes which lead to you feeling unsure, indecisive and abnormal. All of these feelings keep you from doing what you are supposed to be doing.

I strongly believe that if you don't support the moves I am trying to make, then you are undermining them and there is no reason I should be around you. I refuse to let you deliberately or unintentionally mess up what I am doing.

How to win: have game

You win by:

1. Getting away from people stopping you from succeeding

2. Getting away from those who aren't striving for success

3. Getting away from people who aren't supporting your plans

Humans are so vulnerable that the moods, attitudes, ways of thinking, behaving and the bad luck of those we hang around can become our own. If you happen to get snared by a miserable unfortunate you will either spend all your time in a bad mood crying about your circumstances, pointing the finger and engulfed in some bad situation. By the time you realize what's going on you will spend the rest of your time and energy trying to shake that unfortunate person. Miserable unfortunates need to be left in the dust. If they aren't dusted they will eventually roll over and flatten you with blame and misfortune.

People who refuse to better themselves can't assist you either. In fact, they often are haters whose hate surfaces when you are trying to be successful. I can recall when I was on the block selling dope many of my peers were content where they were and with what they had. When anyone from the hood started getting money and made the decision to have more than a high, a bottle and empty pockets those that were content began hating on them. I know plenty of people I considered my friends who wouldn't spend a dime with me unless they absolutely had to. Their actions indicated to me that they weren't trying to help me better myself or my situation. When I went to prison it became crystal clear that I should have moved on from many of the people I considered my friends. They weren't rolling with me they were just in my way.

If your friends aren't supporting your plans, implementing plans of their own and are miserable and unfortunate, they are in your way and need to be rolled over or they will roll over you.

***

Final Word

Think About the Backend

I took this computer class in prison. Before we could move on to anything else we had to learn how to touch type at 40 wpm and be able to pass a technical typing test. The technical typing test consisted of typing several lines of gibberish and special characters in five minutes with no more than five mistakes. I knew how to hunt and peck at around 23 plus words per minute. I figured I could get up to 40 wpm by hunting and pecking and move on.

I didn't tell the teacher that I was going to stick with my two fingered "hunting and pecking" style of typing. Learning to type properly left me typing around 8 words per minute. He must have read my mind because he told me that I would reach a plateau using my style and be severely limited as to what I could do, as far as typing and transcribing was concerned. However, if I learned to touch type, the sky would be the limit. He was right about one thing; I did reach a plateau with my style of typing. I couldn't get over 30 wpm nor could I pass the technical typing test.

I gave in and dropped all the way back down to typing 8 words per minute using the proper typing method. Within three weeks I was typing over 50 words per minute, passed the technical typing test and acquired muscle memory that serves me to this day.

I was focused on the front end. I wanted to reach a goal immediately that would have only had short-term ephemeral benefit. The teacher, on the other hand, shifted my focus to the back end: short term and immediate decline for long term and huge growth. I went from 23 words to 30 using my (front end) typing method and from 8 words to 56 words using the long way (back end method).

My point is: think about how what you are doing now will impact your future. For example, you can work now until you are old for 12 dollars an hour or work for 8 dollars now while you start a business or go to school and earn an unlimited amount of income in the near future. That 12 bucks is the front end but the back end is a current struggle for a far off sunny beach.

Think about the backend!!!

***

www.ingramcontent.com/pod-product-compliance
Lightning Source LLC
Chambersburg PA
CBHW062158270326
41930CB00009B/1574